RELIGIOUS DECEPTION

The Curse of Dead Religion

IVAN STOLZFUS

Printed in the U.S.A.
ISBN Print: 978-0-9965480-0-7
ISBN Kindle: 978-0-9965480-1-4
ISBN eBook: 978-0-9965480-2-1

10   09   08   07   06   5   4   3   2   1

Library of Congress Control Number: 2015910309

Published by:
Stolzfus Books
P.O. Box 108
Pleasant Hall, PA 17246

To Contact the Author:
ivan01kw@gmail.com

CONTENTS

VI | RELIGIOUS DECEPTION

INTRODUCTION

I am not sure at exactly what point of my life my quest for truth began, but it certainly was not until later in life when I finally saw the light. I was born in Gettysburg, Pennsylvania to wonderful parents in a strict Amish community. As a young boy my intentions were always to be a good person. Not once had I ever intended to become the evil person I ended up being.

At seventeen, unable to submit myself to my father's authority, I moved out of my home. I brought my first vehicle and began to exercise my newfound freedom—a life without parental discretion and rules—a recipe for disaster.

My boyhood intentions of being good quickly evaporated and I begin to experiment with drugs. First marijuana, then cocaine and meth. No matter how far I strayed and did my own thing, my soul constantly yearned for a sense of belonging. I wanted solid footing to stand on.

Trying to fill the void and find a place to fit, I began listening to the most evil rock music I could find. I started dabbling in the occult and soon found myself an actively practicing satanic worshiper.

Then one dark night at a party in Dalhart, Texas I received a harsh wake up call. I overdosed on drugs and found my soul hovering above my body. An angel appeared and knelt down beside me, placed my head in her lap, and told me to breathe again. I was miraculously revived ... and terribly shaken. My sin-darkened soul yearned to receive peace. I was desperate.

I began to date the girl who is now my wife. Because we both wanted to get married, we had to make a decision: either join the Amish church or find another church. I had no faith in the Amish, but I joined because it was the only thing I knew how to do. I participated in all the rituals and the mock baptism, but none of the things I did offered real peace or freedom, much less provided victory over sin.

Our first years of marriage were lived in relative peace and quiet, but where sin is swept out but Jesus is not invited in, the demons which return are often as bad or worse than those who were there originally. We begin to drink and live a hard life of wild partying, then suddenly I began to realize that I was on my way to hell. I was thirty-two years old and desperately seeking for an answer. It took me a full year of searching, then Jesus had mercy and lead me through a miraculous conversion experience.

My sinful religious life was immediately changed and I found peace and victory over sin. I experienced real contentment—the very thing I had longed for since the day I had left my home in rebellion and anger. I at last understood why booze, drugs, satanism, and satanic heavy metal rock music could never fill the need for peace. Real heavenly peace can never be found in these things, it can never be experienced by surrendering to any religion.

After my salvation, an onslaught of religious persecution began in full force. Someone gave me a book titled, *1001 Questions And Answers On The Christian Life.* This, they supposed, would change my wayward mind. However, it only served as a tool to drive me even further away from the dead religion that had never offered anyone any hope in the first place.

Religion—this perverted work of darkness—was full of twisted doctrines. Once I realized that there were books like that out there turning people from the truth, I begin to study and dig. I searched and searched some more until the light begin to shine and I began to see a parallel, one that revealed an interesting truth. I started studying, seeking for an answer to my many questions:

- Why do the orthodox Jewish rabbis and the Amish bishops look alike yet profess a different religion?

- What makes the Amish and ISIS favor black clothes and a beard with no mustache?

- What compels the Amish to hate believers of Salvation in Jesus Christ alone?

- Why does ISIS take the greatest of pleasures in killing them?

- What compelled the Jews to kill the author of our faith, Jesus Christ?

- What was it about the Pharisee that Jesus so despised?

- Why do the Amish condemn those enlightened believers like their mother church, the Roman Catholics?

My hunger to know the answers to these questions have resulted in the book you now hold in your hands.

My findings I will now share with you ...

1

Chapter One

THE COST

One of mankind's greatest downfalls is to seek acceptance from family, friends, co-workers, their church, and the world in general. The fact that it is spiritually unacceptable to be well liked by everyone around us makes no sense to a carnally minded man. But Jesus saw for himself how the Gospel of salvation, by grace through faith was rejected. The Scribes and the Pharisees, like many religions and religious people in today's society, could not comprehend anything that was not of this world. They were bound by the traditions and doctrines of men. This was why Jesus was rejected, and so will all men who present the true Gospel of Jesus Christ.

Such rejection has cost thousands of prophets and saints their lives because of the same kind of persecution. Almost from the beginning, because of jealousy, Able, one of Adam's sons, was killed by his brother Cain, the other son of Adam. Cain's anger was kindled because his own sacrifice was rejected and Able's was accepted by God. Cain resorted to what so many ungodly men have done ever since. He lashed out in jealous anger, directed toward the very people who have found favor in God's eyes.

The first sin mentioned in the Bible is disobedience to God. The second one is the rejection and persecution of those who obey Him. Instead of repenting of his own sin and conforming to fit his actions to God's desires, he decided to take matters in his own hands. His punishment, like the one of his father and mother, Adam and Eve, was to be banished from the presence of God.

Many years later, as the world was filled with violence and wickedness, God commanded Noah to build an ark. When he chose to obey God, He was mocked and scorned by his fellow men, yet it was Noah and his sons, the very ones who were persecuted, who were saved from the great flood.

Elijah, the prophet of God, spent much of his life in hiding from pagan idolaters who worshipped at the shrines of Baal. He openly challenged Queen Jezebel and publicly proclaimed what people did not want to hear. His words angered them because they stood against their religion, condemned their idolatry, and pricked their consciences.

The list of those who have been persecuted goes on and on. In fact, several books have been written which record such great persecution. Among those, a large book entitled *Martyrs Mirror*, was written about those early men and women who devoted their lives to God and would not stop for any cause or any man. But the list does not stop with the *Martyrs Mirror*. Neither will it stop as long as there are genuine Christians on this earth.

Early Christians were accused of causing most every calamity imaginable.

Those early Christians were accused of causing almost every calamity imaginable, including earthquakes and pestilence and anything else that could be directed toward them. They were blamed with anything possible to cause others to hate them and bring terror to their lives, or shame to them and their families. They became nothing more than a sporting exhibition to blood-thirsty mobs of people in arenas like the great Coliseum in Rome, and other arenas built by Roman emperors in the early centuries of Christian history. They were thrown into these arenas, some which held as many as 180,000 spectators, often without any way to defend themselves. Starved and frightened wild beasts, whose sole purpose was to tear up those innocent Christians, were loosed upon them, while the crowds cheered and roared with devilish delight.

Yet, they often left this life singing praises to their Lord Jesus Christ, for whose cause they deemed themselves unworthy even to die. They knew, without doubt, that they would soon rest eternally with Jesus. They believed what He had said, that they, his true Christian followers would suffer and be persecuted, as He had.

If the world hate you, ye know that it hated me before it hated you.
JOHN 15:18, KJV

2

Chapter Two

DECEPTION

Through His death and resurrection, Jesus defeated Satan and took from him the keys of death and hell. Satan knew he had lost his reign over mankind, so he began to deceive men once again. This time he instilled the fear of man into their hearts, and so began his reign of terror. He works through those who bow to his evil deception, turning his focus on pagans who worship his images and idols.

Satan convinced men of all sorts of holidays. The Roman population observed as many as a hundred holidays per year, and their celebrations were usually the circus entertainment of the arena, often at the cost of much blood-shed. In fact, there was so much entertainment sponsored by the Roman government that the poor, deluded citizens described their only needs as *panem et circenses* (bread and circus). As is usual, for people who center their lives on pleasure, one thing leads to the next. The Romans led in that category. What once was the highlight of the day soon became boring. Develop such boredom among a horde of pagan idol worshipers and you quickly end up with the early period of such sport—Christian persecution.

It was ever so easy for the dethroned Satan to enter into the scene and execute his new implement of revenge, so easy to shift it into obviously evil man-slaughter. He used another tactic, something even more subtle. He came at those very first Christians in the form of religious priests—the Jewish Pharisees. In that time they were the very ones who had provoked the crucifixion of Jesus, along with the Chief priests and religious leaders.

The Pharisees and scribes were the religious elite. They knew the law very well, yet because of their religious blindness, they had not been able to even recognize Jesus for who He was. He had walked in their midst doing all manner of miracles that only the Son of the most high God would ever be able to do. And now, in the early dawn of Christianity they were determined to eliminate every last one of the followers of the one they had killed. But to no avail. Jesus had had risen again, defeating and making a mockery of death itself.

The years following Jesus' resurrection must have been an extremely anxious time for those Jews. They had bribed the Roman guards who had stood watch over the tomb of Jesus to say that the Apostles had stolen His body. Now, those same Apostles who had followed Jesus were going about preaching, converting others into believing what those Pharisees had tried so hard to exterminate. The Church grew by leaps and bounds. Both Jews and Gentiles were converted to this new belief. They were no longer bound to the law, either of Moses, or of the perverted Jewish traditional law of the Pharisees. (Note: Acts 15:5-11) This claim of salvation by grace through faith was more than their carnal minds could comprehend, or for that matter, what they even wanted to believe. It contradicted the very things they so ferociously had protected, because it was their means of exalting themselves over those they considered to be beneath them. Theirs was a doctrine of men, teachings and restrictions Jesus had condemned.

Now here were these lowly fishermen and publicans following Jesus. Even a few converted Jews, and of all things those despised Gentiles were also following Him. They were refusing to bow to Jewish law any longer. They were following the teachings of Jesus. But the Pharisees and scribes had Jesus' blood on their hands. Thus, the Pharisees, who were under the influence of the devil even before Jesus time, began to do the only thing that they knew. They began to persecute and kill anyone who would not conform to their standards, anyone who dared to teach this new Christian doctrine that contradicted their own. Yet, through their interpretation of their own religious doctrines, they justified the shedding of the blood of those innocent victims.

Actually, the Pharisees did not usually kill the Christians themselves. Instead, they gave them over to the pagan Roman authorities on charges of heresy, or claims of being gods. Such accusations threatened the Roman emperors who presented themselves as be gods and demanded to be worshipped. In the first century, to fall into the hands of the pagan Roman government often meant death, by crucifixion, by being impaled and suspended on a stake, and as entertainment in circus-arena amphitheaters.

John the Baptist, who was the forerunner of Jesus Christ, also preceded him into death. He was beheaded in the castle of Machaerus due to the evil plot of one Herodias. Her foolishness provoked her daughter, Salome, to call for his execution at the hands of King Herod.

Jesus Christ, as we well know, was brutally flogged, spit upon, crowned with a crown of thorns, and crucified. He was nailed to a wooden cross and left hanging there naked to bear unimaginable shame and suffering.

Yet, He did it for mankind's benefit, giving His life for ours. Across the next three centuries, many believers suffered martyrdom as the Gospel spread like wildfire across the Roman Empire. These disciples were usually killed in violent ways, primarily by Roman hands. Indeed, far beyond the first centuries and even to this day, Christians are being slain for their steadfastness of faith. Stephen, a deacon at Jerusalem, was the first believer to be martyred. He was stoned to death outside of Jerusalem in A.D. 34. This was at the hand of the Jews, not the Romans.

All of Jesus' Apostles, with the exception of John, were martyred prior to the end of the 1st century B.C.

- James (the major) was beheaded in Jerusalem—A.D. 45.

- Philip was stoned in Hierapolis—A.D. 54.

- James (the lesser) was stoned and clubbed to death— A.D. 63.

- Barnabas was burned at the stake—A.D. 64.

- Mark died while being dragged to the site of his burning—A.D. 64.

- Peter was crucified upside down—A.D. 69.

- Paul was beheaded after having suffered much imprisonment and persecution—A.D. 69.

- Andrew was crucified—A.D. 70.

- Bartholomew was flogged and then beheaded—A.D. 70.

- Thomas was thrown into a burning oven and pierced through with spears by the natives of Calamina—A.D. 70.

- ❧ Matthew, the evangelist, was spiked to the ground, then beheaded—A.D. 70.

- ❧ Matthias was tied to a cross, stoned, and then beheaded—A.D. 70.

- ❧ The Apostle Matthew was crucified, stoned and then beheaded—A.D. 70.

- ❧ Luke the evangelist was hanged—A.D. 93.

- ❧ Antipas was roasted alive inside a copper steer—A.D. 95.

But this short list of the martyred Apostles of Jesus does not include the hundreds of other Holy Martyrs who were brutally killed alongside the Apostles.

The list goes on and on, and it appears that with the passing of time, more inhuman techniques were employed to persecute and kill Christians. Of course, as time passed many more people were killed for being followers of Christ. It was as though Satan became more determined to extinguish Christianity quickly, before it could become firmly grounded and take root. Those early attempts of Satan were to destroy the Christians by fear and openly brutal tactics in an outward display of violence. This cost the lives of thousands of innocent people, people who refused to renounce their new found faith. But those tactics soon proved futile. Every time one Christian was violently slaughtered it seemed like ten more would boldly rise up out of nowhere to take their place.

Every time one Christian was violently slaughtered it seemed like ten more would boldly rise up out of nowhere to take their place.

It was as though the blood of Christianity served to fertilize the field, producing more and more new Christians. Yet the slaughter continued as Christianity fell prey to an open season of slaughter for anyone who chose to kill them. They were forced to worship in the utmost of secrecy. They often traveled under disguise as merchants, crawled through fields disguised as animals, or met at nighttime and during storms to escape detection.

How very different this was from today's lazy so-called Christians, so many of whom, though they ride to church in fancy heated four wheel drive SUVs, would rather use the weather as an excuse to stay at home. Their lame excuses of, "it's not worth getting killed over" fails to justify their laziness. How strange, since they may well be at a friend's house watching a football game later in the day. That, or they will even find themselves at a stadium. And of course they will be at work the next morning.

People will not go to hell for this sort of behavior. Their actions indicate they are already on their way to hell. Those early Christians had no comfortable houses of worship. They rejoiced to see stormy weather, since that, in itself, lessened their changes of being caught by the authorities.

3

Chapter Three

CONSTANTINE

In time, the Christians separated themselves from the pagan corrupt Jewish Synagogues. They formed their own churches, but persecution seemed to follow them. No matter how often they fled, they could not escape it. For the next almost three hundred years, they suffered extreme persecution. Surely they were weary of being chased about like so many unwanted dogs.

Then, almost as if by chance, a new Emperor came to the Roman seat of power in the year of 306 A.D. He was Flavious Valerius Aureius Constantinus, more commonly known as Constantine I, or Constantine the Great. He was, by most accounts, a religious fanatic, given to all manner of pagan worship.

About 313 A.D. Constantine entered into an alliance with the Emperor Licinius, who was ruler of the Eastern Providences of the Roman Empire. Together, they issued the Edict of Milan, a policy which extended equal rights to all religious groups and freedom of worship for Christians to worship unhindered and unrestrained. Properties, which in times past had been confiscated from Christians, were restored to them. The right to purchase land, and other privileges as well, were also given to followers of Christ. Such privileges had been completely denied before Constantine came to power.

Eventually, Constantine deposed Licinius and became sole ruler of the entire Roman Empire. In approximately 325 A.D. he openly embraced Christianity, although his conversion was primarily political more than anything else. He had not truly found the Lord nor experienced genuine salvation. His actions were only nominal. His actions were taken as an effort to please everyone by uniting all religions into one. He also desired the benefits and blessings that were promised to Christians. He remained very much a pagan god worshiper, and only received Christian baptism on his deathbed. But, the Edict served to give Christians a reprieve from the unrelenting persecution.

The Christians readily accepted their new status, and as one can imagine, the results were disastrous. The doors of compromise had swung open, and in marched the worldly throng of false religions and pagan god worshippers. They brought with them all sorts of strange doctrines, like those recorded in Hebrews 13:9:

> *Be not carried about with divers and strange doctrines. For it is a good thing that the heart be established with grace; not with meats, which have not profited them that have been occupied therein.*

This caused all manner of strife and Constantine was quick to compromise. He gathered a council of 300 bishops from all parts of the Empire to try to resolve the problems. Many religions still follow this practice today, taking matters into their own hands instead of fasting, praying, and seeking the Lord's will. They simply make more rules and go on as before.

It was during this period of time that the Sabbath began to be observed on Sunday. Not only that, but the death of Jesus was soon celebrated alongside the pagan sacrifices to the idol Molech (a Baal), and to his "wife" Ishtar (pronounced "Easter"). Thus, everyone could join in the festivities as common folk without being considered stuck up or odd.

Jesus was crucified during the preparation of the Passover (Note: John 19:14, 31). Passover is a Jewish festival that is celebrated in the beginning of the month of "Nissan." This is the first month of the Jewish calendar, as recorded in Exodus 12. Our calendar was designed and instituted at the direction of Pope Gregory XIII in 1582. This is the calendar followed today throughout most of the world. According to the Gregorian Equivalent this event would be observed around mid-March to early April rather than early to even late April as celebrated by western churches who observe Easter as much as two weeks after the Jewish Passover is celebrated. I point this out not to condemn anyone with respect to their holidays, but to encourage those in these religions to refrain from gossip about or judgment of those who choose not to celebrate these holidays at all. These people, like the Christians of Constantine's time, would rather compromise the truth and turn their backs to it than be considered different.

Christmas is another holiday enshrouded with pagan beliefs. It is unlikely that shepherds would be tending flocks in the night of a Judean winter. It would have been far too cold there on December 25.

Another questionable date that has been the cause of much debate is the observance of the Sabbath day. According to the Bible, Jesus died on the "preparation and the Sabbath drew on" (Luke 23:54). Then on the first day of the week, early in the morning they discovered that the tomb was empty (Luke 24:1). So according to this, Jesus either died on Saturday and rose on Monday (contradicting Christian observance) or, he did die on Friday and rise on Sunday as Christians observe, thus the Seventh Day Adventists are right that the Sabbath is on Saturday. Either way we believe that Constantine also changed the day the Sabbath was to be observed to fit the day his Sun gods—Helios and Apollo—were to be worshiped, Sunday. The good news is that Paul wrote these words.

> *Let no man therefore judge you **in meat**, or **in drink**, or in respect of an holyday, or of the new moon, **or of the Sabbath days.***
> COLOSSIANS 2:16 KJV (EMPHASIS ADDED)

Constantine was probably one of the most significant assets Satan ever used in perverting the early Christian church. Although persecution stopped during his rule, many pagan doctrines, rituals, and sacraments were bought into the church. Thus, it was so badly corrupted that, were it not for the supernatural work of the Holy Spirit, all that Jesus had suffered and died for would have been lost after only 400 years.

Constantine was by no means the only one to carry this guilt. The Christians, who were by this time tired of being martyred and persecuted, chose to follow the world and compromise. They chose the easier, less painful life. Their actions were contrary to Jesus' prophesies, which foretold that His followers would be persecuted (Note: John 15:20). What happened to the churches after this foreshadows what will happen to us if we decide that the real Christian life is too hard. It can happen to us if Christian living is too much bother and we compromise by taking our own route. We must not simply focus on making rules pertaining to dress and other earthly things. We should work toward getting people's hearts right with

We should work toward getting people's hearts right with God—leading people to Jesus for salvation and being filled with the Holy Spirit.

God—leading people to Jesus for salvation and being filled with the Holy Spirit. He is the One who will teach us all things (Note: John 14:26) He does not lead us to form alliances with the world and become their friends just to avoid persecution.

> *If ye were of the world, the world would love his own:*
> *but because ye are not of the world, but I have chosen you*
> *out of the world, therefore the world hateth you.*
> JOHN 15:19 KJV

By far, persecution is more healthy spiritually than compromise. The Holy Spirit is far better at teaching us and keeping us from sins that mere rules. Sins originate from within corrupted hearts, the result of never having been truly born again. We cannot say that we know Jesus if we only depend on some church and its rules to keep us from sin. Jesus said:

> *"I am the way, the truth, and the life: no man*
> *cometh unto the Father, but by me."*
> JOHN 14:6 KJV

Nowhere in the entire New Testament does it teach that we need church-made rules to be Christians. Such belief is a design of the Devil to keep people from experiencing a truly intimate walk with Jesus Christ.

Rules or the law was given to Moses because of transgression (Note: Leviticus 16:16), for the children of Israel because the Holy Spirit was not yet given. But the law did nothing to weed out the root of all evil which lies within man's heart. A new covenant was made (Note: Hebrews 8:7-13), a covenant which writes God's laws into men's hearts.

Satan is a master at religion, and those who follow him are deceivers as well. *"And no marvel; for Satan himself is transformed into an angel of light. Therefore it is no great thing if his ministers also be transformed as the ministers of righteousness; whose end shall be according to their works"* (2 Corinthians 11:14-15, KJV). He will stop at nothing to keep us from the power of the Holy Spirit. But, if we are filled with Him and live in His power, He will keep us in an intimate relationship with the Lord Jesus. Such believers are a major grievance to Satan.

Chapter Four

SEPARATION

The church, as it developed during the reign of Constantine, eventually became known as the Roman Catholic Church. Constantine died in 337 A.D. Soon after his death, the Church turned to persecuting her own people. That is, it persecuted those who found themselves disagreeing with its teachings. Through the influence of man instead of God, the leaders of the Church formed and promoted their own ideas. They decided how things should be done, teaching doctrines that do not match the teachings in the Bible. Yet, these teachings held a resemblance to the Bible. If one did not know better, they sounded very spiritual and holy.

They introduced the baptism of infants. They believed that if one was born in sin, that sin must be washed off in order to enter into heaven. They taught that the bread at communion actually, physically turned into the flesh of Jesus, and that the wine became the actual, physical blood of Jesus. They also taught that a person must confess their sins to a priest in order to receive forgiveness. Priests were believed to have a direct link to God that no one else had.

They established their own kingdom, ruled by their own hierarchical system, which today is headed by the sovereign Pontiff, or Pope. Under his authority are all the patriarchs, archbishops, bishops, apostolic delegates, vicars, prefects, priests, and deacons, as well as the entire membership of the church.

Today's Amish, Hutterites, Mormons, Muslims, and some Mennonites have similar hierarchical systems, though they are not as complex as that of the Roman Catholics. These all contradict biblical teaching. They place men in positions that exalted them above the rest of Church. While Bishops, ministers, and deacons are indeed biblical, this ruler system is not at all what Jesus taught. Even Moses, the servant of God, never took it upon himself to make a single rule. He simply relayed to the people the things which God told him. Nowhere in the New Testament does a bishop, minister, or deacon become a dictator who has the authority to make rules. Rather he is taught by Jesus to become as a servant.

> *But Jesus called them unto him, and said, Ye know that the princes*
> *of the Gentiles exercise dominion over them, and they that are great*
> *exercise authority upon them. But it shall not be so among you:*
> *but whosoever will be great among you, let him be your minister.*
> MATTHEW 20:25-26 KJV

The word minister translates more clearly as servant. This system of dictatorships is a Satanic ploy to take the focus of leadership away from Jesus. It places total control in the hands of power hungry men who are never in short supply, even from the dawn of Christianity. The Roman Catholic Church believes that the Pope is infallible in matters of faith and morals when he speaks EX CATHEDRA. This is Latin for out of the seat, in other words, by virtue of his office. Decrees on these matters, when established by the Pope, or by and with the bishops in council, are considered to be free of error. The Roman Catholics believe that by some spiritual protection of the Holy Spirit, their Church has been kept free of doctrinal error and has maintained the doctrine or teachings of Jesus Christ unchanged. They also believe that it is impossible for error to creep into the official teachings and doctrines of the Roman Catholic Church concerning faith and morals.

In much the same way as the Catholic Church, the Amish believe that because their religion is so ancient, it must surely be considered righteous in God's eyes. Strange, since they also consider the Catholics to be seriously deceived, even though the Catholic church was around some thirteen hundred years before the Amish community was ever formed. The *Martyrs Mirror* quite accurately describes this false sense of justification. It points out that—"Hence it follows, that neither the antiquity, nor the long or great succession of persons, can assure the truth of any religion or church, since the evil is as ancient as the good." (Page 44) The Amish Church, which was considered apostate by the Roman Catholic Church, was founded by Jacob Ammann in the 1690s. This was the result of a division within the Swiss Mennonites. Ammann's forceful teachings served to establish his ideas among a small group of Anabaptist churches, thus the Amish Church was founded by and named after him. At one point in their early history, they excommunicated some five hundred Mennonites who rejected Amman's ideas of doctrine.

In his dominating role as bishop, Amman was not much different from the Islamic prophet, Mohammad. The only difference between Amman's methods and those of Mohammad was that Amman gave his enemies over to Satan. Mohammad simply killed them outright. But, it is important to understand, in most plain religions like the Amish, being given over to Satan is the most extreme condemnation that could possibly befall an individual. If it is done in a biblical setting, it is a serious thing.

But it doesn't give someone the right or the power to simply damn a member to destruction, just because he or she doesn't follow a man-made rule. This is no more right than actually killing people for not accepting one's doctrine.

The state churches of the early centuries, which were controlled by the Roman Catholic Church, practiced both excommunication and the execution of "apostate" members. Actually, the Anabaptist movement originated because of the persecution which was handed out. These hearty souls rejected those man-made and obviously perverted doctrines and suffered greatly because they did.

The Catholic clergy taught and practiced all sorts of superstitious rites and traditional sacraments, teachings which contradicted the true teachings of the Bible. Like the Amish, they could not understand the spiritually discerned teachings of the New Testament because they took matters into their own hands. Those Amish, much like those priests, grieved the Holy Spirit by taking matters into their own hands and taught their traditions, the doctrines of men (see Mark 7:6-9), and the rudiments of this world (see Colossians 2:8). Of course, they would not stand for anyone they deemed inferior to themselves to prove them wrong. They could not let someone expose their dark sin-filled lives they were leading behind their plain clothes. They, being a law unto themselves, and in some cases, being joined together with the kings and rulers of the lands, had free reign in matters pertaining to religion. If they had a public execution planned, so much the better for entertainment

> *… they could not understand the spiritually discerned teachings of the New Testament because they took matters into their own hands.*

purposes. The Catholic controlled state churches normally imprisoned Christians on charges of heresy or witchcraft, and gave them a chance to "repent" and renounce their beliefs. The time allotted a Christian to renounce his faith was about six weeks.

In the Amish religion, a person who is excommunicated will be given over to satan for the destruction of the flesh and then shunned for a minimum of six weeks (see 1 Corinthians 5:5), not unlike the Catholic practice. It does not matter whether the offender has repented for the sin or not. What matters is whether or not the transgression was one of a certain group of sins, or a breach of traditional Amish doctrine. Driving a car, and or other similar actions considered wrong or worldly by the bishops, are punished in this manner. It doesn't even matter whether the transgression is a biblical sin unto death or not. The Amish do not consider repentance as Jesus taught (see John 8:3-11), but will hand members over to Satan regardless.

The strange thing is this: No one has ever figured out how to restore that poor person and bring him back from the grips of Satan. Even though the erring member has served his or her six weeks of man-imposed "repentance," this is left undone. The person will be accepted back in good standing, but the spiritual significance of such a drastic action is ignored.

Many hundreds, even thousands of Christians have been slaughtered, mercilessly martyred for their faith since the time of Jesus. This should not come as any surprise since even Jesus was martyred for the sake of the very Gospel He brought to us. Yet, Jesus Christ, the son of the Most High God, was only one in the line of many who have been senselessly murdered for doing the work of God. Imagine the curse bought on those who condemned and crucified God's only son. Yet Jesus, as he hung there on the cross, patiently, blamelessly, and totally undeserving while enduring the penalty for the sins of world, prayed "Father forgive them for they know not what they do" (Luke 23:34).

The record shows that many of the holy martyrs prayed similar prayers for their persecutors, asking God to forgive them. This should not be surprising. If we are truly filled with Jesus, we will naturally love our enemies. We will bless those who curse us, as did Jesus and the martyrs.

Jesus, while still on earth spoke of the challenge men would face for following Him.

> *Suppose ye that I am come to give peace on earth? I tell you,*
> *Nay; but rather division: For from henceforth there shall be five*
> *in one house divided, three against two, and two against three.*
> *The father shall be divided against the son, and the son against*
> *the father; the mother against the daughter, and the daughter*
> *against the mother; the mother in law against her daughter in*
> *law, and the daughter in law against her mother in law.*
> LUKE 12:51-53, KJV

If all men would accept Him, things would not need to be like this. It is not God's will that there be a division between a father and his son. God did not create it to be so. But Jesus, who could see into the future, saw what His New Testament Gospel message would bring. He so accurately prophesied how it would be as men turned to Him in faith.

This division between fathers and sons comes about because so many fathers reject the truth and then hide it from their sons. What is more, because of the false teachings of lazy or selfish preachers, false religion has become common within the churches. This causes division between those preachers and people who know and follow the truth. Nowhere in the entire New Testament does it say we must all stay in the Church we were raised in as children, even if it teaches false or unsound doctrine. The Bible does teach us, however, that we are not to be "unequally yoked with unbelievers" (2 Corinthians 6:14). Many modern religions teach that any member who leaves must be shunned, excommunicated, or killed. Certainly he or she is doomed to an eternity in hell unless they come back and confess to the clergy. This practice is not limited to the Roman Catholics and the Amish. It extends to the Hutterites, the Mormons, the Islamics, and most known cult groups as well.

How can so many religions, whose teachings vary so greatly in doctrine and belief, all profess to be the only righteous religion while all the rest are wrong? We can then understand why, ever since the time of Jesus, the true church of Christ would suffer persecution. It always has and always will, perhaps with varying degrees of severity, but persecution will occur. Jesus forewarned us—

> *"If ye were of the world, the world would love his own: but because ye are not of the world, but I have chosen you out of the world, therefore the world hateth you. Remember the word that I said unto you, The servant is not greater than his lord. If they have persecuted me, they will also persecute you; if they have kept my saying, they will keep yours also."*
> JOHN 15:19-20 KJV

5

Chapter Five

The Apostate Church

M any Bible prophesies, including Jesus' words, have been fulfilled time and time again. In fact, some of them will never stop being fulfilled until the earth is finally destroyed. That will be the great and terrible Day of Judgment, when Jesus comes to gather his bride from those who have endured until the end. Until that day arrives, we Christians must suffer and endure persecution just like our Lord predicted we would. We should count ourselves privileged even to be counted worthy to bear the cross of suffering for the sake of the Gospel.

> *"Blessed are ye, when men shall hate you, and when they shall*
> *separate you from their company, and shall reproach you, and cast*
> *out your name as evil, for the Son of man's sake. Rejoice ye in that*
> *day, and leap for joy: for, behold, your reward is great in heaven:*
> *for in the like manner did their fathers unto the prophets."*
> LUKE 6:22-23, KJV

So often throughout history, this persecution and killing was brought on by the very ones who professed to be doing it for the sake of righteousness, or for God. All these things they did because they did not know God or understand the Holy Scriptures. If they had understood God's Word and been in contact with Him through the leadership of the Holy Spirit, they would have seen their error and most certainly would not have killed or excommunicated their fellow Christians. But they did, and they still do.

> *They shall put you out of the synagogues: yea, the time*
> *cometh, that whosoever killeth you will think that he*
> *doeth God service. And these things will they do unto you,*
> *because they have not known the Father, nor me.*
> JOHN 16:2-3, KJV

The German phrase is *Sie verden euch in den Bann tun*—"they shall put you out of the synagogues." This word *Bann* is the specific word the Amish use for excommunicate. We all know that to excommunicate an unrepentant sinner is right, even Biblical. It is an abominable thing, however, to excommunicate a person because he leaves a certain church. This is especially true when a church teaches its own man-made doctrine rather than that of the Bible. To excommunicate someone because he has been born again, a transformation which has happened countless times, goes directly against the truths of the Bible. Yet, it is the most common reason the Amish excommunicate people out of the Amish Church. They will not admit this, however. Instead they will usually wait until they can find another reason, some simple offense toward their traditional doctrine, one that has nothing at all to do with any Bible teachings. This is typical, much like the Pharisees did in order to find some fault to crucify Jesus. They used some made up, fictitious fault to achieve their ends.

But having a born again experience is something that many religious leaders cannot understand. Even though Jesus made it clear—

Verily, verily, I say unto thee, Except a man be born
again, he cannot see the kingdom of God.
JOHN 3:3, KJV

How can it be possible that a religion that professes to follow the teachings of the Bible, will excommunicate those who get born again? It can only be that they completely misinterpret the Bible, especially the meaning of being born again.

The Amish interpretation of being born again is to conform to the church rules ... dress, hair styles, and taking some instruction classes for a summer. After that, people are baptized, which in Amish practice is by pouring water over a person's head. No surprise here since they don't have this right either. The Greek interpretation of baptize is to immerse. The Amish mode of baptism, by pouring water on someone, comes from the Catholic Church. It seems fitting that their reason for baptizing should be in line with their mother church. Actually, both churches believe in baptismal regeneration (the washing away of sins through the rite of baptism itself).

This is a deception of the devil, one which takes the focus off of the blood of Jesus Christ and shifts it onto something else entirely. Immersion is the mode of baptism God designed. If we are born again, like Jesus said we must be, we will die to self first, like Jesus did. Then, like Jesus, we will be buried and rise to new life eternal. (Thank God we don't need to be buried in literal dirt!)

When people, in later years of their lives, become truly born again, they find themselves in the same situation their Anabaptist forefathers did. They realize the deception of the church in which they had been members through birth or linage. They often confront the clergy with the truth they have discovered. What follows is an angry onslaught of persecution. They are threatened and challenged to renounce their precious new found faith in Jesus Christ. When they won't recant, their refusal is followed by excommunication, and sometimes it has been followed by death.

At some point, through this complete transformation process—leaving the church and joining another—these new converts often feel a desire to be re-baptized. This re-baptism lies at the root of the word Anabaptist. It was the realization of the error of baptismal doctrine that forced the issue.

The Webster's Dictionary of 1828 offers this definition of Anabaptist:

Anabaptist; n. Gr. again, and a baptist. One who holds the doctrine of the baptism of adults, or the invalidly of infant baptism, and the necessity of rebaptism in an adult age, one who maintains that baptism ought always to be performed by immersion.

So whether or not we were baptized prior to rebirth, either as infants or as adults, we were not properly baptized. In order to properly do the will of God, we must be ana-baptized (again baptized), as the Bible teaches. Throughout the history of Christianity, this doctrine has seen heated debate, with no small fury rising among many apostate churches.

The bottom line is this. The Holy Bible is spiritually discerned. Apostate religions do not follow what the Bible teaches. They have, and always will, come up with their own ideas and turn them into rules and *ordnung*. Then, they enforce them on the membership to prove themselves right. Sadly, many of these religious groups ended up where they are

> **The Holy Bible is spiritually discerned. Apostate religions do not follow what the Bible teaches.**

for the same reason as the Pharisees of Jesus' time. They are blind to the truth. They have created so many rules in their determination to keep the law that they have become separated from the true law itself. The design of their religion was not of faith and not of grace. It was of law. But true Christianity is under the New Covenant, not the law, and it has been so since Jesus' time.

The only religion that maintains even a remote allegiance to the Mosaic Law is Orthodox Judaism. Many other religions, including the Amish, only profess that their doctrine comes from the Old Testament teachings and the laws given to Moses. The strange thing is that so few of their rules resemble that law. And even if they could keep their law to the letter, it would absolutely have no benefit for them.

> *Forasmuch as ye are manifestly declared to be the epistle of Christ ministered by us, written not with ink, but with the Spirit of the living God; not in tables of stone, but in fleshy tables of the heart.*
> 2 Corinthians 3:3, KJV

> *Who also hath made us able ministers of the New Testament; not of the letter, but of the spirit: for the letter killeth, but the spirit giveth life.*
> 2 Corinthians 3:6, KJV

We don't live under the Old Covenant; we are under the New Covenant. Jesus was the center of the Bible and God's plan. Abraham's faith, for example, was in a better covenant and was counted as righteousness because he believed forward. He looked toward the better promise. In other words, he believed in the salvation of Jesus by faith without ever having seen Him.

Even as Abraham believed God, and it was
accounted to him for righteousness.
GALATIANS 3:6, KJV

We, who live in the covenant of the New Testament, believe by faith, exactly like Abraham did. The difference is that we look back in time and by faith. Though we have never actually seen Jesus, yet we believe on Him for salvation by faith. What we must realize is that if we try to return to the old law for anything pertaining to righteousness, we are actually looking past the Lord Jesus. And this is exactly what Satan would have us do.

And not as Moses, which put a vail over his face, that the children of
Israel could not stedfastly look to the end of that which is abolished:
But their minds were blinded: for until this day remaineth the same
vail untaken away in the reading of the old testament; which vail is
done away in Christ. But even unto this day, when Moses is read,
the vail is upon their heart. Nevertheless when it shall turn to the
Lord, the vail shall be taken away. Now the Lord is that Spirit: and
where the Spirit of the Lord is, there is liberty. But we all, with open
face beholding as in a glass the glory of the Lord, are changed into
the same image from glory to glory, even as by the Spirit of the Lord.
2 CORINTHIANS 3:13-18, KJV

This is why so many religions do not have a clear picture of grace through faith. They hold fast to and believe in the old law with its list of rules. Then they reject salvation by grace through faith. Though many would have you believe otherwise, these two do not go together. There is absolutely nothing in that old law which brings us to salvation. The law merely serves to give us the knowledge of sin to bring us to Christ.

For the law made nothing perfect, but the bringing in of a
better hope did; by the which we draw nigh unto God.
HEBREWS 7:19,KJV

The first covenant, or the law, was not perfect, yet it ushered in the new covenant which is through Jesus.

For if that first covenant had been faultless, then
should no place have been sought for the second.
HEBREWS 8:7, KJV

So many religions miss this whole concept completely. Faith in Jesus alone doesn't make sense to them. Like the Pharisees, they try to help things along by adding their own ideas of what salvation should be. The result—mass spiritual death.

This is what happened to the Pharisees and what happened to the Roman Catholic Church in the third century. The truth was compromised when Constantine's ideas of how things should be done were accepted. Still, Constantine's ideas were no more wrong than the Amish *Ordnung*, because it was much easier to discern wrong from right then. The Amish *ordnung* has no divine ordinance in it, no notion that God forgot to add to the law. There is nothing that makes it sufficient for salvation.

Wherefore then serveth the law? It was added because of
transgressions, till the seed should come to whom the promise was
made; and it was ordained by angels in the hand of a mediator.
GALATIANS 3:19, KJV

The mediator alone is sufficient for salvation and Amish preachers will nearly all acknowledge that their *ornung* will not get them to heaven. So, why then do they excommunicate those who leave them? They hold no hope of salvation for those whom they have excommunicated. But since they have turned them over to Satan, they don't seem to care.

Actually, they do believe there is salvation in their doctrine. They see their standards as having redeeming merit. Truthfully speaking, we do need some standard, some moral righteous belief structure to keep us from sinning. Certainly the law is meant to hold us until we have come to Jesus for redemption and have been filled with His Holy Spirit. But the Spirit is the One who will teach us all things, not the elders. (See John 14:26.)

> *Wherefore the law was our schoolmaster to bring us unto*
> *Christ, that we might be justified by faith. But after that*
> *faith is come, we are no longer under a schoolmaster.*
> GALATIANS 3:24-25, KJV

It is hard to imagine how any religion that is so far detached from the Holy Spirit actually believes they have the power "to deliver such an one unto Satan for the destruction of the flesh, that the spirit may be saved in the day of the Lord Jesus" (1 Corinthians 5:5, KJV). Yet, if we look back at the foundation on which they were established, the doctrine of Jacob Ammann, there is no reason to wonder. Men just cannot help adding confusing rites and doctrines when the Holy Spirit is not involved. Over the centuries there have been many who found the truth, many who tried to share it with the bishops and preachers in the Amish Church. Almost all of them have been excommunicated and strictly shunned. This ordinance was prescribed by the prelates to keep the truth away from the rest of the church. Otherwise, everyone would see the truth and prove the Amish doctrine to be apostate.

6

Chapter Six

REJECTION OF JESUS

Nearly all orthodox religions have rejected Jesus in much the same manner as the Pharisees did. His Gospel is far too different from the doctrine to which they have submitted themselves. The Pharisees were no worse in this sense than the Amish, the Mormons, the Catholics, the Hutterites, and even many Mennonite religions. They did not reject His teachings any more than these religions of today's world do. Almost all of them have rules by which they control their members. Many of these pertain to clothing and hair style. The rules are the fruit of their lives, fruit that shows just how far they have fallen from God and the Gospel of Jesus.

Take, for example, the rule about wearing a hat. The Bible clearly teaches—

> *"Every man praying or prophesying, having his head covered, dishonoureth his head."*
> 1 CORINTHIANS 11:4, KJV

*"For a man indeed ought not to cover his head, forasmuch as he is
the woman is the glory of the man."*
1 CORINTHIANS 11:7, KJV

These verses should not require much spiritual discernment to
understand clearly. It simply says a man indeed ought not to cover his
head. He does not need to wear a hat to show God is his covering.

While there is nothing sinful in wearing a hat for protection against
extreme elements, it does not matter that some long-ago forefather wore
one. Neither is it significant that someone taught some doctrine about a
man wearing one. The Bible clearly teaches against it. So, for a religion to
impose rules on its membership concerning hats is not biblical. How a hat
must look, be shaped or worn, and that beyond any question, a hat must
be worn to church has no basis in the Bible. Yet, in the Amish Church, if
a man refuses to wear a hat to church, he will soon be excommunicated.

This doctrine is only one among many others that show how completely
and thoroughly these religions have rejected Jesus. This is because His
doctrine does not line up with theirs. In the same way, His doctrine
did not line up with the Pharisees either, while He was still on earth.

*They know
about Him,
but they do not
know Him.*

The reason their doctrine does not line up with
His is because they do not know Him. They
know about Him, but they do not know Him.
Knowing about Jesus is no great thing. Even
the heathen acknowledge the deity of a supreme
God. "Thou believest that there is one God; thou
doest well: the devils also believe, and tremble"
(James 2:19, KJV).

Another dark side that comes out among the Amish is the misuse of
authority. They are prone to excommunicate almost anyone, just because

they want some violation of their rules "swept under the carpet." They really don't want to deal with such things.

We read in John, chapter 9, that the Pharisees did much the same thing. Jesus had healed a man that was blind from birth. When he refused to discredit Jesus or his healing, they dealt with the problem by casting him out of the synagogue.

> *They answered and said unto him, Thou wast altogether born*
> *in sins, and dost thou teach us? And they cast him out. (i.e.,*
> *excommunicated him) Jesus heard that they had cast him out;*
> *and when he had found him, he said unto him, Dost thou believe*
> *on the Son of God? He answered and said, Who is he, Lord,*
> *that I might believe on him? And Jesus said unto him, Thou*
> *hast both seen him, and it is he that talketh with thee. And he*
> *said, Lord, I believe. And he worshipped him. And Jesus said,*
> *For judgment I am come into this world, that they which see*
> *not might see; and that they which see might be made blind.*
> JOHN 9:34-39, KJV PARENTHESIS ADDED

The Pharisees were furious with Jesus because He had violated their Sabbath rules. When He spit into the dust, stooped down and made clay, he was "working on the Sabbath. It would have been acceptable if he had only spit on a stone, but to spit in the dust to make clay, on the Sabbath was forbidden. In the Jewish oral law, making clay was an act of labor, one that made something usable to build.

One of the most beautiful aspects of this story is that Jesus came back after He had heard that the Pharisees excommunicated that man and saved his soul. He condemned those Pharisees because they were without Biblical justification, not that they were in the least bit concerned about that. They had their own doctrine which they held to be higher than the words of Scripture. It is interesting that the Amish follow their example, almost to the letter.

So many religions today twist Scripture and use it to fit their doctrine rather than to make their doctrines to fit the Scriptures. They do this because there is no biblical justification for man-made church rules. The Scripture teaches against such rules, calling them traditions and doctrines of men, or commandments of men. In other words, they are church rules and are clearly not in the Bible. Jesus did not teach us that we need to make rules and *ordnung*. Neither did the apostles.

> *He answered and said unto them, Well hath Esaias prophesied*
> *of you hypocrites, as it is written, This people honoureth me with*
> *their lips, but their heart is far from me. Howbeit in vain do they*
> *worship me, teaching for doctrines the commandments of men.*
> *For laying aside the commandment of God, ye hold the tradition*
> *of men, as the washing of pots and cups: and many other such*
> *like things ye do. And he said unto them, Full well ye reject the*
> *commandment of God, that ye may keep your own tradition.*
> MARK 7:6-9, KJV

The Apostle Paul wrote much of the New Testament. He also taught against church rules, warning against anyone who tried to teach them.

> *But even if we, or an angel from heaven, preach any other gospel to*
> *you other than what we have preached to you, let him be accursed.*
> *As we have said before, so now I say again, if anyone preaches any*
> *other gospel to you than what you have received, let him be accursed.*
> GALATIANS 1:8-9

Most church rules take on a form of godliness, but are actually the design of Satan to take one's focus off of Christ rather than on Him. This is how they would have you believe. Here is another of these rules, these regulate the wearing of beards. Some churches teach against any facial hair at all. Their men must be clean shaven. Another church teaches that men must wear a full untrimmed beard. Yet, they are not allowed to wear a mustache. If God requires men to wear beards, what does He prefer, a full beard or something different? Should there not be some teachings in the New Testament to indicate what He desires?

We know He gave instructions about beards in the Old Testament, but He also allowed the "eye for eye, and tooth for tooth" rule. Furthermore, He required blood sacrifices to be offered for sin. He also forbade the complete gleaning of fields and vineyards so that the corners would be left for the poor. (see Leviticus 19:10) This teaching is not followed by today's religious farmers. Neither is the law concerning hybrid produce.

Ye shall keep my statutes. Thou shalt not let thy cattle gender with a diverse kind: thou shalt not sow thy field with mingled seed: neither shall a garment mingled of linen and woollen come upon thee. (Leviticus 19:19, KJV) If this passage of Scripture were observed no Amish farmer would be allowed to farm with mules. Just consider this scenario: an Amish farmer, plowing his field with a team of mules, with part of his beard shaved and trimmed, and wearing a denim (cotton) coat with a wool lining. Every aspect of that picture is a violation of the Levitical law (of Moses).

Even though they try to observe the Old Testament laws, they break them in so many ways. It makes no sense. And according to the Bible, breaking that law is sin.

> *For whosoever shall keep the whole law, and yet*
> *offend in one point, he is guilty of all.*
> JAMES 2:10, KJV

This word law, as used in this passage, literally means the Old Testament law. The teachings of the New Testament offer no such bondage. How a beard is worn has nothing to do with a man's salvation. If a man trims his beard because of his pride, or if because he assumes a certain type of beard will not help or improve the work of salvation, that man is already in sin. The condition of the heart is the only thing Jesus requires to be kept a certain way. How people dress, wear their hats, or trim their facial hair is of no consequence. What they drive or ride in has nothing to do with getting one's heart right with God. Jesus taught us that we should: "Judge not according to the appearance, but judge righteous judgment" (John 7:24 KJV).

Satan loves to fill our lives with "feel good about myself" ordinances. They might make us look reverent and feel holy, yet the Bible teaches us that: "Wherefore by their fruits ye shall know them" (Matthew 7:20 KJV). These fruits of a Christian do not include, or even mean, clothing. The Pharisees also believed their clothes would draw them into righteousness. But they didn't.

> *But all their works they do for to be seen of men: they make broad their phylacteries, and enlarge the borders of their garments.*
> MATTHEW 23:5 KJV

If a religion bases its principles on the law, they will perish. Look at the many variations found in so many religions just regarding the beard. If there were anything about a beard that pertained to righteousness, either the Mennonites or all the Amish would all go to hell, because their doctrines contradict each other. Yet they both strongly teach their individual doctrine as being right and pure.

The Bible does not present a multiple doctrine. And the truth is this; they are both wrong. They base their religion on earthly things, not spiritual things. Those who say they don't believe their doctrine is for salvation need to start living it out by letting those who see the light go free and clear. By punishing those who leave your apostate religion for not keeping your "commandments of men" simply proves you to be liars. John 3:16-18 does not include the notion of *ordnung*, and versus 19-21 perfectly describes those elders, bishops, popes, mullahs, and rabbis who enforce rules on born again believers. There is no difference in those religions, whether they be Catholic, Islamic, Mormon, Amish, Mennonite, Jewish, or Hutterite. They all teach a form of law that must be observed. All of them are wrong. All of them have added to, or taken away from the Holy Scriptures to fit their own ideas of how things should be done.

> *Desiring to be teachers of the law; understanding*
> *neither what they say, nor whereof they affirm.*
> 1 TIMOTHY 1:7 KJV

7

Chapter Seven

PERSECUTION

For most of its history, the Bride of Christ has been under persecution. This has served to keep it pure and without spot or wrinkle (Note: Ephesians 5:27). Simply put, lukewarm Christians are not able to withstand the trials of persecution. Being a part of the bride of Christ is not an easy life. Neither was one promised. The rewards are not in this time, but in the eternal times to come. One promise we do have though is: *"I will never leave thee nor forsake thee"* (Hebrews 13:5). We are promised victory over sin and temptation, but not an easy life, as many would have us believe. Those who try to have a Christian life while making their life easy are wasting their time. Being accepted by the crowd is not the way of Christianity. Neither is depriving oneself of certain things others do or have somehow count for righteousness. God certainly does not count it that way.

We cannot help it if the Gospel upsets people, and we will not stop presenting it to those we meet just because we don't want to upset them. That is not to suggest that we should use the Gospel for that purpose. We must not try to bring persecution on ourselves or use the Gospel only for arguments so we can feel good about ourselves. Upsetting other people is not our purpose. Still, some people we meet, for whatever reason, do get upset. Some even become vehement when the truth of the Gospel is presented to them. The reason they take offense is because they are guilty— living in sin. When they are presented with the Gospel, they are faced with a choice, one they are unprepared to face. They must choose, either to accept or reject the teachings of Jesus Christ. To accept means they must admit to themselves that they are wrong and must repent of their sins and accept Jesus as their personal Savior. Their only alternative is to reject Jesus, His Gospel message, and His salvation.

This is something many people are not prepared to do. Deep down inside they might realize they need Jesus to save them, but they are not ready or willing to accept Him or follow His teaching. Therefore, their most common reaction is anger, and their response to a Gospel encounter is to make the evangelist feel like he is the one in the wrong. Those people who know they are living in sin do not want to face up to it.

The root system of all persecutions: anger, hatred, enmity, strife, pride, all fruits of evil

This is the root system of all persecutions: anger, hatred, enmity, strife, pride, all fruits of evil (see Galatians 5:19-21). The Bible says people such as these will have no part in the kingdom of God (see Galatians 5:21). Most of those who become angry when they are presented with the truth are either lukewarm Christians, or they are under conviction and are yet unwilling to repent. So their obvious reaction is to lash out in anger against the most obvious thing that is bringing them under conviction. That is the person who is presenting the Gospel of Jesus to them. If people are truly on fire for God, they will rejoice when they are presented with the teachings of their Lord and Savior Jesus Christ. No real Christian will be angry when another Christian, a fellow laborer in the Lord, is presenting them with the true teachings of the Bible.

The teachings of Jesus angered the Jews and Pharisees of Jesus time, the Romans directly after His time, the Roman Catholic Church in the early centuries, and various corrupted religions even until this day. Governments, kings, and religious clergymen have all been convicted of their sins and been angered by those who were responsible for bringing them the truth. It was for this reason that Jesus was crucified and His true followers have suffered ever since. Today's world is no exception whatsoever.

The true teachings of Jesus Christ have also caused many religions to persecute those members who confronted the clergy with the Gospel. What they failed to see is this. The way they behaved toward true Christians exposed them for who they really were deep inside. They were not Christ-like, even though they convinced themselves and others that they were. Rather, they were ravening wolves, covered in sheep's clothing. They were not leading people to Christ. They were using Christianity to justify their dictatorships. No part of the bride of Christ would excommunicate or kill its born-again believers. Just think about this. This is about as far removed from Christ as one could possibly be.

In whom the god of this world hath blinded the minds of
them which believe not, lest the light of the glorious gospel of
Christ, who is the image of God, should shine unto them.
2 CORINTHIANS 4:4, KJV

Satan has those apostate religions so wrapped up in his confusing deception they won't even stop to consider what they are doing. They do not have the ability to see that the victims of their persecution are only doing what Jesus taught. Because of this, they are being treated exactly as He said they would be. Jesus said that the world loves its own. They will not hear us for the same reasons they have not heard Him. They will also hate and persecute us for the same reasons they persecuted Him (see John 15:18-20). It is because they chose to follow the world rather than Jesus Christ.

8

Chapter Eight

THE UNGODLY FOREFATHERS

One of the great misconceptions of our time is this. Whatever the old forefathers did and taught is sacred and holy. This fallacy originated within the Catholic Church which considered its patriarchs as saints, having no regard whether they were ungodly and immoral while they were still alive.

The Amish put huge emphasis on the divine righteousness of the *aldi*—the "old ones," or forefathers of the church. They teach that because these are the way they did things, these ways must be right. Never once do they stop to consider the teachings of Christ. Neither do they compare the teachings of the forefathers with those of the Bible to see if they are different. Obviously they are, or the Amish would not have ended up where they are today. A prime example of this is found in the way they still use and teach from the Apocryphal books. These were once thought to be part of inspired Scripture.

Websters 1828 dictionary; APOC'RYPHA, n. Gr. from, to conceal. Literally, such things as are not published; but in an appropriate sense, books whose authors are not known; whose authenticity, as inspired writings, is not admitted, and which are therefore not considered a part of the sacred canon of the Scripture.

Jewish rabbis and scholars (and later early Christians) determined which books of the Bible were divinely inspired and thus adopted into the "canon" of Scripture. The remaining books that did not make it into the canon were called apocryphal and generally accepted as good historical and religious documents, but not equal to the Hebrew Scriptures. To this day, the apocryphal books are received by the Romish Church as canonical, but not by the Protestants.

The translators of the King James Version removed those books because they simply did not belong there. They were added by the Roman Catholic Church as a way to justify their perverted teachings. Sadly, the Amish continue to teach from them. Their wedding sermon is based on a story found in the book of Tobit. This is a story about a young man who is sent out by his father to collect a debt. He meets an angel who serves as his guide. They stop to camp, and young Tobit becomes frightened when a large fish attacks him, apparently charging out of the water at him. The angel guide advises him to catch the fish by the fins and pull it out of the water. Then he instructs him how to preserve various organs of the fish, including the heart, the liver, and the gall. He is to use these in the future to drive out demons. Thus, this insight would later become useful to the young Tobit.

When Tobit arrived at his destination, he met with the man from whom he was to collect the debt. It was discovered that they were related, and the angel proposed a marriage between Tobit and the daughter of the debtor. This is where things become somewhat demonic. The angel warned Tobit that the reason this girl was still single and a virgin was because she had been "kidnapped" by the demon Asmodeus. This demon would not allow any man to be with her and take her virginity because he was jealous. She had been married seven times, but each time the married couple went into the wedding bed, the demon killed the groom before he could take her virginity.

The angel instructed Tobit that he was to make a smoke offering using an "ash of perfume" from the heart and liver of the fish that had attacked him. Then he would be able to safely possess his new bride without fear of the demon killing him. Tobit did as he was instructed and made the ash. As they entered the bridal chamber, he offered up the smoke sacrifice. The demon, Asmodeus, smelled the smoke and fled into the uppermost corners of Egypt where the angel bound him.

This is the theme story of the Amish wedding, taken from the context of a book not even found in the Bible. Of course, they do not describe every detail of this story. Rather, they change it somewhat to make it sound less demonic. How crafty Satan is to influence church leaders to use such ideas. Jesus did not teach the use of fish organs offered up as smoke sacrifices to cast out demons. Neither do we need to use such examples to inspire weddings or any other sermons in the era of the New Testament.

While the Tobit story may be an interesting one, maybe even a true one, the question remains: Is that the closest thing that the Amish can find to a Godly wedding sermon?

The Old Testament has many beautiful stories that can be used as good sound wedding sermon material. Take the story of Isaac and Rebecca for instance (See: Genesis 24). Through his prayers, Abraham's servant was able to find God's chosen wife for his master's son, Isaac. This is just one example of many wedding stories that could be drawn from Scripture. While these are not as elaborately described as some of today's weddings, the moral behind the stories is truly beautiful. Even the Tobit story has some good points. Yet, might it be a design of the devil to use some apocryphal story to inspire a wedding sermon? Why not use one that is inspired by God, one taken from the true Bible? (See 2 Timothy 3:16). Failure to do so denies the newlyweds of a blessing that would come from a beautiful, Holy Spirit inspired wedding sermon.

Many of the Amish do not even realize that the Tobit story is not found in the King James Version (KJV) of the Bible. They would be shocked if they knew the entire story. The books of Sirach and Maccabees are others of the apocryphal writings from which some of the Amish preach. They do this, believing that since the forefathers did it, it is good to continue doing so. This is a deception of the devil however, designed to preserve the darkness they bought upon themselves by continuing to follow the traditional rituals of the Catholic Church. They do not seek God's will through fasting and prayer. Neither do they seek His will for a godly church. Instead, they do what the Christians did in the third century when they accepted Constantine's ideas and those of the pagan god worshipers of the world. They sat down together and decided among themselves what they thought would be a good way to do things. But that was a compromise with the written word of God.

Today, they are so indoctrinated they do not even know how to correct an errant doctrine, even if they see the error in it. They would rather patch up problems with their own ideas than seek God through fasting and prayer. Actually, they do fast and pray. They fast by skipping breakfast twice a year, on dates prescribed by the Church prelates. They pray using prayer books, or offer completely silent prayers, rather than crying out to God from the depths of their souls. They have Church every two weeks with absolutely no Bible studies or prayer meetings. Gatherings such as prayer meetings and Bible study are, for the most part, strictly forbidden. In some districts, teaching German in school is forbidden as well, for fear the children will grow up to understand too much of what is being taught. Then they would see the error in their doctrine and leave the church.

Satan has his cancerous evil deeply rooted in this dark religion indeed. German is the language used in the churches and few understand enough of it to get any teaching from the Bible at all. Long recited prayers are often chanted in a sing-song way, a way designed by Satan to lull people into a sleepy trance so they get nothing out of it. Without even realizing it, the Amish have fallen back into the same dead religious rut as the Roman Catholics from which their forefathers originated, some five hundred years ago. Their determination to use a language that few understand is no different than the Roman Catholic Church which used Latin until 1965. So is the preaching from the apocryphal books and the sing-song way of preaching and reciting prayers. Reciting prayers out of prayer books is also a tradition originating in the Catholic churches.

The clergymen within the Catholic churches have been rife with darkness. Sins such as homosexuality and child molestation continue to be discovered. But many of the plain religions are faced with the same problem. There are countless cases of hidden child molestation among the plain religions. Today, more than ever, women and girls, men and boys are coming to the light, admitting that some relative, hired hand, neighbor, uncle, brother, father, or grandpa, had sexually molested them as children or youths. In some cases, the offender is deceased and will never have taken any opportunity to repent. These are the all too obvious fruits of dark sin within a religion, especially when they are "swept under the carpet" rather than confessed.

Many children have grown up, tormented with literal visible demons that were let into their homes because of the dark hidden sins of their fathers. Many have gone through life suffering, never having a real conception of the sacredness of undefiled sexual relationships in true Christian marriage. It is easy to look into the lives of the unmarried Roman Catholic priests and see how evil some of their lives have become. Why are we unwilling to see it when it is in our own communities and our own lives? The Amish lifestyle looks attractive to the "work-worried" throng of the worldly minded. They see a quiet, peaceful people content to live without modern conveniences and ways. In many ways they are. But some of the plain religions in today's world are nothing more than Satan dressed in sheep's clothing.

The deception of plain clothes has been taken too far. It is time for someone to stand up and become a voice of truth, regardless of the cost. These people are living in some of the darkest sin since Christianity came into the world. They have become a subtle, demonic, false religion which offers a false sense of righteousness. This is the most powerful trap that Satan has ever been able to set. It has slain more innocent victims than any other. The Roman Catholic Church has become too obviously defiled over time to be truly effective for what Satan desires to happen with Christianity. So he has planted his banner in the very churches that only five hundred years ago, separated themselves from the corrupted Roman Catholic Churches.

Having grieved the Holy Spirit, they do not even feel their need for Him anymore.

Now, so many people have fallen asleep, lulled by an easy life in the great American dream. This dream offers freedom of religion, lots of money, and many material things to have and to do. But it has lost all contact with God. Having grieved the Holy Spirit, they do not even feel their need for Him anymore.

Most of the "plain religions" in America today don't even know Who the Holy Spirit is or what He is about. They don't know what purpose He serves in the lives of real truly born again Christians. Very few churches know the real meaning of fasting and praying to seek God's will. Rather, they have chosen the way of death. They have compromised God's will by taking matters and problems in their own hands. They have added a rule here or there, abolished this thing or that, and ordered everyone to wear certain clothes. Absolutely none of these has any influence on the condition of a soul that is spiritually dying within. Neither do these rules offer any hope of salvation, even though that is what they supposedly do. It is a Satanic plan to offer a false sense of righteousness—self-righteousness without the grace and mercy of God.

9

Chapter Nine

RULES OF DEATH

There is a problem with religious rules. They make a way for people to hide from their guilt. If they were forced to answer to God, rather than to men, they would feel the weight of their sin. But instead, a sinner can hide quite comfortably in religion if he is only responsible to appease the prelates of the church. Ecclesiastical punishment of tradition and *ordnung* does nothing to change the condition of the heart. True, it may cause an individual to abandon a particular sin by the willpower of the flesh. This is how the Old Testament law worked. However, it does little, if anything, to change the condition of the heart, where the roots of the problem lie.

If you want to rid the vegetable garden of weeds you don't simply cut them off, you pull them completely out of the ground. That leaves no chance of them sprouting again from the same root. This is how sin must be removed from the heart of man. It must be removed from within, not merely cut off from the outward man. (See Matthew 3:10). That's what the Apostle Paul meant when he wrote about the circumcision of the flesh. Circumcision of the flesh is vain; it is the circumcision of the heart that profits a man's soul. Under laws there are always loopholes. Then, more laws are needed to close those loopholes, but new laws simply create new loopholes. Eventually, the entire fabric of the law ends up as a bunch of patches sewed upon patches, and fences built around other fences. What really needs to be done is to destroy the enemy. Then no fences will be needed!

Members of a church who have sin they struggle to overcome do not need harsh rules enforced on them as a path to victory. Neither does medication (pharmaceuticals) offer victory over sin. In fact, the term witchcraft is closely connected with the word *pharmakia* from which the words pharmacy and pharmaceuticals are derived. Furthermore, is it not very likely that they need some counselor to talk them out of their sin. What they need is to be truly born again. It is not being conformed only to the church rules that changes people. It is being transformed by Jesus Christ. That is the way to righteousness, being truly repentant of all sins, broken-hearted before Jesus, and committing one's entire life fully to Him. This, and this alone, is how anyone will find true victory over the roots of evil. To be truly born again is to be given a new heart, a redeemed heart from the only One who can give it—Jesus.

We cannot perfect the flesh by obeying a set of rules that are not even mentioned in Scripture. Struggling sinners often hate their sins as badly as anyone else. They may find short term victory in trying to do better. Eventually they will either fall back into the same sin, or Satan will give them over to some other sin, one that makes them feel better about themselves. Their response might be "I don't use drugs anymore, I was able to quit, so now the worst thing I do anymore is smoke a little pot." Or maybe they don't drink hard liquor anymore, only beer.

This is no victory whatsoever. It is deception from the devil. True victory does not trade one sin for another. True victory is complete deliverance from all bad habits and sins in our lives. Real victory like this is only possible through Jesus Christ, not through any church or its rules. A church and its born again membership may be instrumental in leading a sinner to Christ for the redemption He offers. But salvation is not in the church itself, neither is going to church by any means sufficient to bring someone to Christ. We must first realize that we are lost, and there is no other way we will ever be saved but through Jesus Christ.

> *Neither is there salvation in any other: for there is none other name under heaven given among men, whereby we must be saved.*
> ACTS 4:12, KJV

We are not our own masters. We will always be serving one master or another, either God or Satan. We cannot be the masters of our own lives. It is impossible. If we decide to follow Jesus, we will suffer persecutions. We may well lose family and friends. Sometimes true converts are so severely shunned they lose all contact with their relatives and relationships. They become as dead to those they were once close to, nothing more than painful memories lost to time. While such loss is hard, it does not cause true Christian converts to forsake their faith, even though those people who excommunicate them reject them. In some satanic way, they would like for their satanic design to force true believers to recant. But excommunication and shunning work in the opposite way. These methods cause converts to reach out to Jesus and to other like-minded believers.

Our ungodly forefathers bought this design of the devil out of the Roman Catholic Churches when they left so many years ago. And the Roman Catholics followed the way of the Pharisees. They did so even though they were unaware of what they were doing. They did not totally renounce the dead religious rituals and sacraments of the past. They did not completely abandon that from which they came in order to embrace true faith in Jesus Christ. Rather, they continued to rely on their own ability to resolve the problems that arose. They chose to resort back to what they were used to in their former church and its way of resolving problems and issues. They continued to cast out anything or anyone which was confrontational or disagreed with their doctrine.

Excommunicating, shunning, persecuting, killing—making rules against true Christians does not cause them to go away or be quiet. It seems to be beyond any real possibility for these hierarchical systems (like Pharisees, Roman Catholics, and the Amish) to accept correction and repent. They have become gods in their own minds, exalting themselves far, far above the lay membership. They will not accept the truth when it comes from anyone they deem to be inferior to themselves. They come across as being

> *Making rules against true Christians does not cause them to go away or be quiet.*

sorrowful after they have freshly excommunicated another Christian. They use this method to "warn" the rest of the church of the dangers of being deceived. Then, they threaten people with the punishment of hell.

How ironic, that the church leaders become Satan's messengers to persuade people to follow the doctrine of the church and its forefathers rather than that of Jesus. Satan loves religion. Those innocent victims of his deception, who out of the fear of man and their version of excommunication, are bound by the very religion they assume is from God. But by seeing someone given over to Satan and the condemnation of hell, most people would not dare to question such doctrine. This doctrine of excommunication is preached freely, condemning those who have found the truth and left the church.

The prelates become desperate, frantic when someone questions them about their doctrine. Their favorite, actually their only justification, is "that is the way the forefathers did before us." Often they will add, "Do you really believe they all went to hell?" That is a tricky question. It forces a person to judge the dead forefathers, but it is designed to cause a person to feel guilty for even having such thoughts. Yet in their hearts, these same preachers offer no hope for any of the Catholics, the church from whence they and their forefathers came. They are too blinded by their own deception to see that they are no different than the Roman Catholics they so despise.

Were it not for the emotions behind their sermons, no one would have any reason to believe them. They present themselves as austere and reverent, with long beards, long plain hair, and wearing big black hats. Often, their heads are bowed, as though they were under a tremendous burden for all the wicked sinners. They seem to carry the weight of those among them who very shortly will be told of the torment of burning in hell with the devil and all his angels. But these, without a doubt, include all who do not follow the doctrine of the *aldi*.

These preachers of church rules and *ordnung* look contrite. They give the impression that they are divine messengers with humble countenances, men who live in complete separation from the worldly throng. In their way of preaching their speech is modest, trembling, and full of contrition. Their eyes are closed as if in deep meditation. You can sense the inward fear and apprehension, the tear-filled eyes, the throats choked with emotion, least they would lead anyone astray.

The sad thing is they really believe they are doing it all for God, and those who follow them agree with them. But, they do not follow the teachings of Jesus and His apostles in the New Testament. Instead, they compare themselves and their doctrine with their forefathers and judge according to tradition.

> *Forasmuch as ye know that ye were not redeemed with corruptible*
> *things, as silver and gold, from your vain conversation received*
> *by tradition from your fathers; But with the precious blood*
> *of Christ, as of a lamb without blemish and without spot:*
> 1 PETER 1:18-19, KJV

Jesus' own words describe them well.

> *Woe unto you, Scribes and Pharisees, hypocrites! for ye are like*
> *unto whited sepulchers, which indeed appear beautiful outward,*
> *but are within full of dead men's bones, and of all uncleanness.*
> *Even so ye also outwardly appear righteous unto men, but within*
> *ye are full of hypocrisy and iniquity. Woe unto you, Scribes and*
> *Pharisees, hypocrites! because ye build the tombs of the prophets,*
> *and garnish the sepulchers of the righteous, And say, If we had*
> *been in the days of our fathers, we would not have been partakers*
> *with them in the blood of the prophets. Wherefore ye be witnesses*
> *unto yourselves, that ye are the children of them which killed the*
> *prophets. Fill ye up then the measure of your fathers. Ye serpents,*
> *ye generation of vipers, how can ye escape the damnation of hell?*
> MATTHEW 23:27-33, KJV

No one more perfectly fits this category than those plain dressed bishops who lament those evil churches that slew the martyred forefathers for their faith in Jesus. Then, they follow the same pattern, excommunicating and strictly shunning their own sons and daughters, those whose only desire is to follow their Lord Jesus. They reject and persecute those who seek to be unhindered by their defiled church doctrine.

This is one of Satan's most devious devices, causing people to be afraid of coming to the true light rather than following man-made rules. Satan knows the Gospel of Jesus better than you or me. He has had two thousand years to sharpen his skills. Without guidance from the Holy Spirit we do not stand a chance against his wiles of religious deception. His design is to rob the newly converted of their new found faith. He portrays it as having little importance compared to the teachings of the religious forefathers. He wants people to believe it is far more important to get their hair and dress right with the church standards. If they do, the rest will follow. But the rest never does. What happens is that these rules rob people of their faith in Jesus, which alone will bring with it the living salvation. It is not the outward adorning of plain clothes, but the inward surrender to Christ that changes a man's heart. Our faith in Him alone is what will stand the test of fire by which our deeds will be tried.

Satan hates the new life we can have in Jesus. So, he tries to convince us that we must now surrender our lives to a plain church. Their rules will keep us holy and righteous. But that denies us the power of the Holy Spirit, which was sent of God to teach us all things (See John 16:13). Think about this. Where in the New Testament does it teach that we must submit to church rules? Where does it teach that we need them to keep us close to God? It doesn't.

Liars will try to convince you that the rules are the answer. They will often use Bible verses to do this. But the truth is—

> *Christ hath redeemed us from the curse of the*
> *law, being made a curse for us: for it is written,*
> *Cursed is every one that hangeth on a tree.*
> GALATIANS 3:13, KJV

But if ye be led of the Spirit, ye are not under the law.
GALATIANS 5:18, KJV

*But we know that the law is good, if a man use it lawfully; Knowing
this, that the law is not made for a righteous man, but for the
lawless and disobedient, for the ungodly and for sinners, for unholy
and profane, for murderers of fathers and murderers of mothers,
for manslayers, For whoremongers, for them that defile themselves
with mankind, for menstealers, for liars, for perjured persons, and
if there be any other thing that is contrary to sound doctrine;*
1 TIMOTHY 1:8-10, KJV

10

Chapter Ten

THE COMMANDMENTS OF MEN

The carnal man needs rules to keep him from doing evil. We are to submit to the laws of the government. We are commanded by Jesus to pay taxes. If there were no laws in this world, people would not stop at intersections. There would be no speed limits enforced to keep us driving at a safe rate of speed. Murderers and robbers would have free reign, and the whole world would be in chaos.

Laws can be good, as Paul writes in 1 Timothy 1:8-10. But those churches which have unscriptural church rules, *ordnung,* or even "brotherly agreements," have little restraint. Ministers and bishops would greatly benefit from spending more time on their knees seeking wisdom from the Lord than worrying over irrelevant things like how someone is dressed, or how and why they wear facial hair. True, people should dress modestly, for Scripture states that to be true. If they would begin to preach life rather than some dead religious ritual taken from tradition, things would change. If they preached by the inspiration of the Holy Ghost people would be born again. They would too. This would produce Holy Spirit led Christians who could become free from the law.

We will never make it to heaven in any other way, no matter how righteous our outward appearance looks to man. If we are born again, we should not still be trying to make it into heaven by subjecting ourselves to some form of law. When we do, we are demonstrating that we place greater faith on the commandments of men than on faith in Jesus Christ (See Galatians 3). Yet, thousands of religious and worldly ministers and bishops are in their positions simply because they were ordained by chance—lottery, or the casting of lots as they call it. Selection is done in these ways because they do not know the power of the Holy Spirit.

Others have some seminary degree and have been hired to preach. Still others, through their own selfish ambitions, would have you believe that they have been called by God. They probably believe that themselves. But if they do not know God, how can they know He has called them?

The godlessness of so many religious groups is apparent. They know no other form of righteousness than that which is taken from the world from which they pretend to separate themselves. Thus, they make rules about every little thing. They do this to try to help them be more righteous, which is exactly what the Pharisees did. But Jesus spoke out against all of these things, and His message remains clear today. The Amish, and many other religions as well, have so many rules they have lost contact with the very One they profess to serve. Everything has become ritual instead of God's grace.

There is no life giving power, no leadership at all from the Holy Ghost. If ever there was, it is certain this is no longer so. So many religions have turned their backs on the Holy Spirit because they do not understand Him. Neither do they understand His purpose, which is to teach us all things. His indwelling presence took the place of the law given to the Jews. So many religions have started to pursue the ways of the Spirit, but because of peer pressure, try by their own power to be baptized with or filled with the Holy Spirit. Instead of subjecting themselves to fasting and prayer and seeking God as the apostles were instructed to do, they opened their souls to the spirit world without God. This allows many counterfeit spirits, demonic beings from the devil, to come in. Satan is only too anxious for them to go into the spirit realm. He will fulfill their desires and show them deceitful lies. The Holy Bible teaches us to try the spirits to see what their origin really is.

> *Beloved, believe not every spirit, but try the spirits whether they are*
> *of God: because many false prophets are gone out into the world.*
> 1 JOHN 4:1, KJV

Speaking in tongues or prophesying is not proof that someone is truly filled with the Holy Spirit. Neither should the fear of being led by a counterfeit spirit from Satan provoke a reaction against the Holy Spirit of God. Quite the opposite, for only through the leadership of the Holy Spirit will any church group or individual remain true to Christ across the test of time.

Across time a religious group may continue to function, but their fruits will become corrupted. They will begin to teach strange doctrines. Their youth may turn to worldly pleasures, become promiscuous, yield themselves to experimentation with drugs, and run afoul of legal authorities. To counter such problems, many of these churches simply make more rules, most of which directly contradict true Bible teachings. Of what spiritual value is demanding that clothing have no buttons? Or how a hat should be worn? On what scriptural premise does the color of a cigarette hang? Why should the color of one cigarette be acceptable while all others are sin? And these are merely three examples of the binding rules which have nothing to do with faith, Scripture, or one's relationship with God. They are corrupted fruit, harsh laws to keep people bound to a system that has lost its way.

The Roman Catholic Church, since early in history, baptizes infants. Any true Christian should be able to see straight through this corruption. That was one of the principal issues that separated the Anabaptists from Catholicism in the first place. Why then can these same self-proclaiming Christians not see through such absurd rules?

> *In whom the god of this world hath blinded the minds of them which believe not, lest the light of the glorious gospel of Christ, who is the image of God, should shine unto them.*
> 2 Corinthians 4:4, KJV

This blindness places these people exactly where Satan wants them —lawless workers of iniquity, in respect to the God given Mosaic law without the Holy Spirit to lead them (See Matthew. 7:23). They depend wholly on the leadership of man to interpret the Scriptures for them.

Ministers and bishops are to watch over our souls. Promoting such laws and rules does nothing to protect the souls of people. Rather, these laws give people a false sense of righteousness. But Satan himself is the author, not God. To be sure, these bishops and ministers use many Scripture references to defend their teachings. But there are none which truly justify them.

> *And consider that the longsuffering of our Lord is salvation--as also our beloved brother Paul, according to the wisdom given to him, has written to you, as also in all his epistles, speaking in them of these things, in which are some things hard to understand, which untaught and unstable people twist to their own destruction, as they do also the rest of the Scriptures.*
> 2 Peter 3:15-16, NKJV

For when they speak great swelling words of emptiness, they allure
through the lusts of the flesh, through lewdness, the ones who have
actually escaped from those who live in error. While they promise
them liberty, they themselves are slaves of corruption; for by whom
a person is overcome, by him also he is brought into bondage.
2 PETER 2:18-19, NKJV

These verses describe religious deception to the letter. There are many passages and chapters you will never hear uttered in an Amish Church. They, like many other constitutional religions will not preach from the entire Bible because it contradicts their belief. They teach that their rules are sacred and holy in the same manner the Jews taught their "oral law." Anyone who dares to contradict these "commandments of men" will quickly be excommunicated and strictly shunned. When a man is excommunicated, his wife is not allowed to ride in the buggy with him unless she drives the horse. Neither is she allowed to have any intimate contact with him for the six weeks or more that he is set aside from the church for punishment. No one is to have any business dealings with him. No one may receive any object or money from his hand. No one is allowed to eat at the same table with him.

These are just some of the restrictions intended to pressure him into "repentance." While excommunication, and even shunning come from a biblical perspective, the way these constitutional religions use them is not. They use these to punish an unrepentant sinner, or worse, to punish a born again Christian who questions the corruption with-in the church. These actions are no different than the Pharisees or the Roman Catholic Church that these religions profess to disagree with. The Amish, like the Catholics, do not believe that certain sins can be forgiven unless they are confessed through the church system. This is an insult against the blood of Jesus.

While confessing our sins and repenting to those who have been affected is certainly good and biblical, it is not a reason for excommunication. It certainly is not sufficient evil to cause someone to be handed over to Satan for the destruction of the flesh (See 1 Corinthians 5:5) The Amish clergy is a hierarchical system, and is no more righteous than that of the Roman Catholics. Both systems are controlled by dictatorial leaders who deny individual members the opportunity to follow the leadership of the Word of God. In some form or other, many of the Roman Catholic beliefs and rituals have found their way into the Amish system. They are the results of ambitious men who long to become great rulers within the Church. The only way they can do this is by making rules, then convincing the membership through deceptive teaching. This is the only possible explanation for "strict church rules" in which members are excommunicated for not observing their rules.

> But Jesus called them unto him, and said, Ye know that the
> princes of the Gentiles exercise dominion over them, and they
> that are great exercise authority upon them. But it shall not be so
> among you: but whosoever will be great among you, let him be
> your minister; And whosoever will be chief among you, let him be
> your servant: Even as the Son of man came not to be ministered
> unto, but to minister, and to give his life a ransom for many.
> MATTHEW 20:25-28, KJV

It is impossible for any constitutional religion that enforces rules in their church system to explain these three verses away. They are Jesus' own words. If Jesus, who is the Bishop of our souls, did not come as a ruler but as a minister (servant), why should any sinful man exalt himself into such a position?

The results have been disastrous. Mass spiritual death occurs when men assume dominating positions of rule over others. Thus they deny the Holy Spirit any chance to lead individuals to be truly in tune with God. Even Moses did not rule, but led as God instructed him. Neither did he make a single rule, but received the entire law from God.

Mass spiritual death occurs when men assume dominating positions of rule over others.

The Amish did not receive their rules from God. They made them all up themselves, and did so in the same way Constantine did. They gathered with other men to decide for themselves how things should be handled. The Amish, Mennonites, Mormons, Huterites, Muslims, Catholics, and Pharisees all scoff at each others' "perverted" doctrines. Yet, they don't see how they themselves are utterly perverted. There is none that is better or worse than the other. It never fails, when men begin to lose touch with God and grieve the Holy Spirit, their fruits become very obviously corrupted. Then He no longer is able to lead them. Little wonder they make rules of their own.

The coming of the lawless one is according to the working of Satan, with all power, signs, and lying wonders, and with all unrighteous deception among those who perish, because they did not receive the love of the truth, that they might be saved. And for this reason God will send them strong delusion, that they should believe the lie, that they all may be condemned who did not believe the truth but had pleasure in unrighteous
2 THESSALONIANS 2:9-12

Chapter Eleven

BAPTISM

B aptism is a Christian Sacrament. It is detested by Satan, and he has swayed clergymen in some of these religious systems to pervert it, to hide its true intended form and meaning. This is just another result of the compromise between leadership by the "commandments of men" and being led by the Holy Ghost. But He, and not they, will truly teach us in all things. (See John 16:13) Baptism means to immerse—pure and simple.

Strong's Greek Dictionary 907. aptizo (bap-tid'-zo); from a derivative of NT:911; to immerse, submerge, to make whelmed, (i.e. fully wet) used only in the New Testament of ceremonial ablution...

Webster's 1828 Dictionary [A-J] immerse IMMERSE, v.t. immers'. L. immersus, from immergo; in and mergo, to plunge. 1. To put under water or other fluid; to plunge; to dip. 2. To sink or cover deep; to cover wholly; as, to be immersed in a wood. 3. To plunge; to overwhelm; to involve; to engage deeply; as, to immerse in business or cares.

The Amish and the Catholics both teach baptismal regeneration. This is the false belief that the act of baptism washes away sins. But that is not true. Only the blood of Jesus Christ can ever wash away sin. Baptism is a Christian rite that signifies that we have died to self, are buried (thus immersed in water) with Jesus in baptism, and are risen, made new to live with Jesus.

> *Know ye not, that so many of us as were baptized into Jesus Christ were baptized into His death? Therefore we are buried with Him by baptism into death: that like as Christ was raised up from the dead by the glory of the Father, even so we also should walk in newness of life. For if we have been planted together in the likeness of His death, we shall be also in the likeness of His resurrection: Knowing this, that our old man is crucified with Him, that the body of sin might be destroyed, that henceforth we should not serve sin.*
> ROMANS 6:3-6, KJV

Therefore, the Greeks when they read their Bibles would understand Romans 6:3-4 like this: *"Know ye not, that so many of us as were **immersed** into Jesus Christ were **immersed** into his death? Therefore we are buried with him by **immersion** into death: that like as Christ was raised up from the dead by the glory of the Father, even so we also should walk in newness of life"* (KJV, words altered and emphasis added).

The English word "baptize" originated from the Greek word "*baptizo*" Those who insist on pouring on as their mode of baptism have made all sorts of empty pretexts why pouring is the biblically determined mode of baptism. None of these make any sense at all. One only has to look at the word baptize and immediately realize that immersion would certainly be the biblical mode. But then, since they believe in baptismal regeneration, what difference does it make if they also use the wrong mode of baptism? Here is a biblical reference to baptism which indicates how this rite took place.

*And he commanded the chariot to stand still: and they went
down both into the water, both Philip and the eunuch; and he
baptized him. And when they were come up out of the water,
the Spirit of the Lord caught away Philip, that the eunuch
saw him no more: and he went on his way rejoicing.*
ACTS 8:38-39 ,KJV

It is hard to imagine why two men would have gone down into the water and then came up out of it have a cup of water poured onto one of their heads. It is equally as hard to image why John the Baptist would have gone down into the River Jordan to scoop up water with a cup and pour it on people as well. When Jesus was baptized, he came up out of the water (See Matthew 3:16). It only makes sense that if Jesus came up out of the water, He first must have gone down into the water as well. Surely there would have been at least one person in the crowd polite enough to go down to the water's edge to fetch a cup full of water to baptize Jesus if this is how it was to be done.

So many religions try to make the Scripture fit their doctrine rather than making their doctrine fit the Bible. Perhaps this also explains why they are totally blinded to the truth.

*In whom the god of this world hath blinded the minds of
them which believe not lest the light of the glorious gospel of
Christ, who is the image of God, should shine unto them.*
2 CORINTHIANS 4:4, KJV

Jesus never sinned. If baptism truly is the washing away of sins, Jesus would never have needed to be baptized. But Jesus, before he took up the reins of ministry, died to His own will, and submitted publicly to the will of the Father. He signified this to all men by dying to self, being buried in baptism. He arose, fully surrendered to the will of His heavenly Father who sent Him. In like manner, we are to surrender to Him who died for our sins. He paid our ransom price with His own blood, redeeming us from eternal death which was brought on us by sin. When Jesus died on the cross, blood and water flowed from the spear wound in his side (See John 19:34).

> *And there are three that bear witness in earth, the Spirit, and the water, and the blood: and these three agree in one.*
> 1 JOHN 5:8, KJV

The blood provides for our ransom from sin, the water for baptism, and the Holy Spirit is our seal. All of these bear witness of Jesus Christ. Satan, who was defeated by Jesus' most gracious act of self sacrifice, hates anything that pertains to the life we can have in Christ. He has convinced many religious leaders that baptism needs not be what it was intended to be. Many constitutional religions have adopted pouring or sprinkling as their modes of baptism.

Satan hates anything that pertains to the life we can have in Christ.

If we look at their fruit, we can see that this is but one of the sacraments they have defiled. They do so by adding their own ideas to them. The reasoning they offer for adopting "pouring on" rather than immersion is typically and universally the same. They speak of it as the manner in which the Holy Ghost was "poured on" to each one. Of that reasoning, I would ask, "Does the Holy Ghost only touch our head? Or, is He given to fill our whole being with the presence and guidance of God?" Other common reasons for pouring on are that "it's less messy," or "it can be done year around, even in cold weather" or "it's easier for the old folks." Pitiful excuses for not following biblical truth. What has happened to taking up one's cross to follow Jesus? Suppose Jesus had decided that it was "too uncomfortable" to be stripped naked on a cold night, to be whipped to a bloody pulp, then led into some garbage dump to be nailed to a wooden cross.

The Christian life requires some personal sacrifices and that includes a cross. A cross is not a fancy little painted affair hanging on some church wall. It represents a lifestyle of self sacrifice. There are very few Christians today who have even the remotest understanding of this concept. The plain religions are no exception and are not much different in their way of believing than the Pharisees were in Jesus' time. Nor does God respect them any differently.

God is no respecter of men and the Gospel of Jesus never changes. Jesus gave his life and shed His own blood for redemption of sin.

> *In whom we have redemption through His blood, the forgiveness of sins, according to the riches of His grace.*
> EPHESIANS 1:7, KJV

> *And from Jesus Christ, who is the faithful witness, and the first begotten of the dead, and the prince of the kings of the earth. Unto Him that loved us, and washed us from our sins in His own blood,*
> REVELATION 1:5, KJV

Baptism does not wash away sins. Neither does it signify the washing away of sins. It signifies that we have surrendered our entire lives to our lord and master Jesus Christ. We are not surrendered to religious laws, as the Amish will have people believe. They have taken the holy sacrament of baptism and changed its meaning to cause their members to pledge their allegiance to the Amish Church. They have changed the sacredness of the blood of Jesus, which cleanses us from our sins, into a perverted form of baptism. Common tap water has been substituted for the Blood of Jesus.

> *Of how much sorer punishment, suppose ye, shall he be thought worthy, who hath trodden underfoot the Son of God, and hath counted the blood of the covenant, wherewith He was sanctified, an unholy thing, and hath done despite unto the Spirit of grace?*
> HEBREWS 10:29, KJV

12

Chapter Twelve

ANOINTING WITH OIL

*Is any sick among you? let him call for the elders of the
church; and let them pray over him, anointing him with
oil in the name of the Lord: And the prayer of faith shall
save the sick, and the Lord shall raise him up; and if he
have committed sins, they shall be forgiven him.*
JAMES 5:14-15, KJV

Very few churches practice this sacred rite anymore. They would
rather put their faith in doctors and modern healing practices.
Doctors and hospitals have their place … always have. But modern
American Christians seem to have lost all faith in the truth of the Bible.
They would rather turn to a doctor than to some old fashioned Bible
verse. They complain about rising health care costs. They worry about
the new health care laws. Yet, their faith in the healing power of Jesus
Christ has become so weak one would think they have adopted Judaism.
You would think they do not even believe Jesus is alive at all. Either
that, or somehow over the course of time, Jesus must have grown weak
and shrunk into the background instead of standing at the forefront of
Christianity.

If the truth be told, this is exactly what seems to have happened in the lives of many of the Amish people. Their faithlessness is demonstrated by their actions. The deeply saddening thing is that they have placed their faith in the healing powers of sorcery and witchcraft. Their ignorance has blinded them, yet their ignorance continues because they have chosen to hate true Christians and their beliefs. They will not let themselves be told the truth because they have become self righteous and proud. They grow angry when they are presented with the Gospel.

> *Having the understanding darkened, being alienated*
> *from the life of God through the ignorance that is in*
> *them, because of the blindness of their heart:*
> EPHESIANS 4:18, KJV

This blindness, this faithlessness, has turned an already corrupted society even further from the Jesus they have forgotten. His name is only uttered when absolutely necessary, or when the preachers use it. That is only in church, only when necessary, and only by the preachers. These modern, alternative healing techniques stem from the most ancient of forms of Satanic healing practices—incantations and spells which were performed by tribal shamans, witches, mediums, and sorcerers. People of today, and especially plain people, are flocking to these modern witches in droves, seeking to be healed through methods which are obviously questionable. This age of yoga, "feel good, connect with your inner self" so called Christianity will fall for anything, as long as it professes to be Christian. Yet there is absolutely no sense of discernment between Satanism and Christianity.

Jesus never needed to perform muscle testing, pow-wowing, black boxes, pendulums, or irisology ... just to name a few of the popular healing practices found in modern day witchcraft. Neither did His disciples. And neither do His true followers, even two thousand years later. Jesus is very much alive today and is as powerful and willing to heal as He has ever been. True healing power is given to those who seek Him. In fact, healing is an awesome way to convince sinners that our Gospel message is higher than any other and our God greater than any god ever worshiped.

Have you ever noticed how those people who go to these questionable doctors are never quite healthy? Do not be deceived. Satan has no true healing power. He has the power to move pain around in one's body. For example, he might change a head ache into a stomach ache or a back spasm into a sore leg. His victims always believe healing is just around the corner, and that as soon as a "doctor" figures out what is needed, the problem will be healed. Yet they steadily sink deeper and deeper into a quicksand of dark depressing illnesses until they feel utterly hopeless.

Don't be deceived. Modern witches don't dress in black robes or wear black pointed hats. They don't live in dark secluded woods, ride on brooms, or necessarily have black cats. They do not stand behind big black kettles cooking potent, foul-smelling, spell casting brews while the moon is full. These satanic witches live in and among the communities around you. They go to church, shop at the local markets, and converse in everyday language. Their children attend the local schools, sing in the church choir and play with the neighbor children. They have nice offices in town with bright lights and friendly receptionists. There is soft seductive music playing somewhere in the background, which puts

Satanic witches live in and among the communities around you.

people at ease and calms any fears and dispel any doubts you may have developed since you read this.

The days of Satan coming on as a roaring lion are over, and no marvel.

> *Satan himself is transformed into an angel of light. Therefore it is*
> *no great thing if his ministers also be transformed as the ministers*
> *of righteousness; whose end shall be according to their works.*
> 2 CORINTHIANS 11:14-15, KJV

Those fairy tale books that so-called Christians have purchased so plentifully for their innocent little children, books about goblins and scary witches, are a cunning design of the devil. They prepare your children to look totally in the wrong places for evil. They make such spiritual evil look like a silly fairy tale, just for the little ones. There is no witch living in the dark woods, no house made of candy and gingerbread to lure innocent little children into her liar. Neither is there a troll living under a bridge. In fact, there is no such thing as a troll. Yet the real witches of the third millennium are living in your midst. They go to your church and minister death to you and your children. They are dressed as kind, innocent, and totally harmless people—Amish, Mennonite, Hutterite, or worldly, church going folks.

Let us look at some definitions of words in the Holy Bible. Sorceries; (See Revelation 9:21).

Strong's Greek Dictionary 5331. pharmakeia (far-mak-i'-ah) from 5332; medication ("pharmacy"), i.e. (by extension) magic (literally or figuratively):--sorcery, witchcraft.

Sorceries (See Acts 8:11) means; "magic" sorcery. Magic means; magic, (art) sorcery. The use of charms, spells, and rituals in seeking or pretending to control events or govern certain events or certain natural or supernatural forces; occultism. Such charms or spells etc. any mysterious seemingly inexplicable or extraordinary power or quality.

Magic is the general term for any of the supposed arts of producing marvelous effects by supernatural or occult power and is figuratively applied to any extraordinary seemingly explicable power. If anything would describe some of the "natural" healers and their techniques, it would certainly be sorcery. The Bible gives no hope whatsoever to those who are involved in sorcery. The term witchcraft includes—

> *Idolatry, witchcraft, hatred, variance, emulations, wrath,*
> *strife, seditions, heresies, envyings, murders, drunkenness,*
> *revelings, and such like: of the which I tell you before,*
> *as I have also told you in time past, that they which do*
> *such things shall not inherit the kingdom of God*
> GALATIANS 5:20-21, KJV

If you practice any of these questionable healing techniques, you seriously need to reconsider where you are headed. These powers may seem innocent enough, but they are not. You should be praying out loud, in the name of the Father, the Son, and the Holy Spirit, while you are being "doctored." Then you will be able to discern between good and evil, because Satan will not be able to work his magic in the presence of the Trinity.

However, this question remains. Why would anyone need to go through all those dark rituals for healing when pure simple childlike faith in Jesus can heal us? Anointing with oil and praying in faith is unmistakably a biblical standard of healing. The oil, of itself, is not to be credited for the healing. But just as baptism in water is a God given sacrament that signifies we have committed ourselves to God, being anointed with oil for healing and by receiving healing prayer, we place our faith in God. We line up our faith with His written word and believe that it is true. We will not always be healed immediately (for reasons we may not know), but this should not discourage us. We should continue to believe Him and persist. Jesus taught this in the parable of the unjust judge.

> *And there was a widow in that city; and she came unto him, saying, Avenge me of mine adversary. And he would not for a while: but afterward he said within himself, Though I fear not God, nor regard man; Yet because this widow troubleth me, I will avenge her, lest by her continual coming she weary me. And the Lord said, Hear what the unjust judge saith. And shall not God avenge His own elect, which cry day and night unto Him, though He bear long with them?*
> LUKE 18:3-7, KJV

When we anoint with oil, we do our part—which is to pray in faith, knowing that our Lord is able to heal. Doing this, we know we are doing the will of the Lord. Then we are to leave it at that. Too many people have lost faith. They feel condemned, if there are no immediate results after an anointing ceremony. However, we are not called to do the healing, that is God's responsibility, to His honor. To be real, sometimes healing is not instantaneous. Sometimes there are reasons far beyond our human understanding, but that is not to say we should have, or even can have an attitude of doubt. To excuse our doubts by saying "if God wants to, He can heal" is not what we should do. It is true, in that He is the one who heals, but that is not our decision. We are to believe and obey. When Jesus heals, He heals. Saying anything less may well be making an excuse for our faithlessness. We are called to obey Him in faith and wait for the fulfillment of His promises.

It seems that for every great work of God, Satan comes along with a counterfeit to offer us. All the dark powers of witchcraft are those counterfeits of Satan. One of the main reasons people do not experience wonderful healings through anointing is because they have more faith in their well-stocked medicine cabinets than in the Bible. The only reason they are anointed is to gain attention. Perhaps they are hoping for a moment of fame should God happen to heal them. Those who are unwilling to abide any form of witchcraft as an option must rely completely on God's healing. Those who have no access to medication or who refuse to take them must also rely on God's healing. Those who cry out to God in desperation are most often the ones who experience healings through anointing and praying.

Satan has a counterfeit to offer everyone. He is the author of all lies and deception. He is quick to offer his services to anyone willing to believe them. To the flesh, they may seem more pleasing, and they seem more scientific than an ancient rite like anointing with oil. But they are not in the Bible.

Satan is the author of all lies and deception.

For those who like to dabble in the spirit world, or play with magic, don't worry. Satan will be most pleased to accommodate you on your way to destruction. If you believe that you or your "doctor," that person who doctors you using these questionable healing techniques, are not in this category, you're wrong. If you somehow have fallen into this snare, you can escape. Just remember, God is no respecter of persons. He does not hold you, or me, any higher than the next person.

As long as someone denies the fullness of Jesus, they will have no power to discern right from wrong. Doctors, spiritual healers, and questionable healing practitioners are no exception. They may seem right, but they are not.

There is a way that seemeth right unto a man,
but the end thereof are the ways of death.
PROVERBS 16:25, KJV

13

Chapter Thirteen

THE BANN
EXCOMMUNICATION

A church that excommunicates its born again believers will never have any of them become leaders This becomes the pride of Satan's domain. Jesus was crucified on charges of heresy. Hundreds, perhaps thousands of our Anabaptist forefathers were burned at the stake on charges of heresy. Today, heresy is one of the most common charges used against Amish people who come to the full assurance of their salvation.

Heresies—Webster's 1828 Dictionary [A-J] heretic HER'ETIC, n. A person under any religion, but particularly the Christian, who holds and teaches opinions repugnant to the established faith, or that which is made the standard of orthodoxy. In strictness, among Christians, a person who holds and avows religious opinions contrary to the doctrines of Scripture, the only rule of faith and practice. 2. Anyone who maintains erroneous opinions.

The Amish often refer to a born again believer's faith as "a strange belief." If that individual refuses to renounce their belief and make it fit alongside Amish Church doctrine, they will be excommunicated. While it is biblically justifiable to reject heretics, *"A man that is an heretic after the first and second admonition reject"* (Titus 3:10, KJV). So the determination must be made, who is really the heretic?

Perhaps some of these old order religions, including the Amish and Hutterites, should stop to consider their own doctrine, Perhaps they should determine whether or not they might be the ones who are wrong before they excommunicate others on charges of heresy. One should not assume that the antiquity of a religion validates it as pure. The evil is as ancient as the good is and the Bible should be the measure.

The Roman Catholic Church, which all plain religions agree is evil, is much older than the Amish, the Hutterites, and the Mennonites by more than a thousand years. So the theory that antiquity proves righteous accuracy is a sham. Jesus did not say "by their age ye shall know them." He said "by their fruits" we shall know them, and their fruits have become seriously corrupted. Although they excommunicate anyone who disagrees with their doctrine, those whom they excommunicate are like those Jesus described and prophesied about nearly two thousand years ago.

> *They shall put you out of the synagogues: yea, the time*
> *cometh, that whosoever killeth you will think that he*
> *doeth God service. And these things will they do unto you,*
> *because they have not known the Father, nor me.*
> JOHN 16:2-3, KJV

To put someone out of the synagogues is the same thing as putting someone under the *bann*. This is the German word attached to "casting out from the synagogue," or more accurately to "excommunicate." Yet, it seems they would rather continue this injustice than to be proven wrong. They become infuriated if someone dares question their doctrine. Indeed, the Amish have become the Pharisees of the third millennium.

The Pharisees rejected the teachings of Jesus. They also refused to accept correction. They could not see that they were no longer keeping the true law, but rather were keeping their own law. These were the laws they had made up to help them maintain Jewish tradition, yet they were not observing the true law of God. Because of this, they were spiritually blind, blinded by their own self righteousness. If they had kept and observed the laws and correctly interpreted the prophesies of the Bible, they would have been able to receive Jesus when He came.

So it is with the Amish. If they would keep the commandments of Jesus rather than their own version of righteousness made to look like righteousness, they would be able to see those who are truly born of Christ. If they had not mixed just enough of the Bible into their rules to make them look authentic, they would accept corrections and find delight in the Gospel. Sadly, this will never happen. It never did to the Pharisees—the Orthodox Jews. Nor has it happened to the Roman Catholic Church. Yet, God in His great mercy has made it possible that those who are open to His truth will see it. He will be faithful to deliver them up from the bondage they are living in.

> *And I say unto you, Ask, and it shall be given you; seek, and*
> *ye shall find; knock, and it shall be opened unto you.*
> (LUKE 11:9, KJV)

Jesus said we will be persecuted.

> *Remember the word that I said unto you, The servant is not greater*
> *than his lord. If they have persecuted me, they will also persecute*
> *you; if they have kept my saying, they will keep yours also.*
> JOHN 15:20, KJV

He did not say that we might be, or could be persecuted. He said we will be persecuted. He was talking to His true followers, those who have the fruits of righteousness coming forth from out of their lives, those who keep his commandment.

> *These things I command you, that ye love one another.*
> JOHN 15:17, KJV

> *For this is the message that ye heard from the beginning, that we should love one another.*
> 1 JOHN 3:11 KJV

If Christians are true and have the fruits of truth in them, they will love one another. They will be considerate of one another. They will love their brethren enough to see and then accept Godly correction. Persecution is God's way of keeping His flock pure.

> *And these are they likewise which are sown on stony ground; who, when they have heard the word, immediately receive it with gladness; And have no root in themselves, and so endure but for a time: afterward, when affliction or persecution ariseth for the word's sake, immediately they are offended.*
> MARK 4:16-17,KJV

> *And these are they which are sown on good ground; such as hear the word, and receive it, and bring forth fruit, some thirtyfold, some sixty, and some an hundred.*
> MARK 4:20, KJV

The definition of persecute is to torment, harass, condemn, or to inflict unjust punishment for religious reasons. Ultimately, persecution can lead to death as well. How similar to the *bann*, that strict Amish shunning, where they teach that to be excommunicated from their church is certain condemnation to hell. That is, of course, unless one repents and comes crawling back to the prelates in humble submission to them. Their way of keeping their membership is not by evangelizing and accepting members from those they deem heathen. It is to raise their own membership from their own children.

From the cradle, these children are taught that they have been born into the church God wants them in. To leave would be certain condemnation to hell. To do so would be breaking God's first commandment, which is "Honour thy father and mother …" (See Exodus 20:12), and that would be an absolute, no-way-out decision. Actually this is not the first, but the fifth commandment. Without question, this is a commandment of God, and it should be obeyed as long as we live. Yet, it does not mean to obey that which is sinful or wrong, especially in blind faith.

The Hebrew definition of "honor" is—

Strong's Hebrew Dictionary 3513. kabowd (kaw-bode'); kabod (kaw-bode'); a primitive root; to be heavy, i.e. in a bad sense (burdensome, severe, dull) or in a good sense (numerous, rich, honorable; causatively, to make weighty (in the same two senses):--abounding with, more grievously afflict, boast, be chargeable, X be dim, glorify, be (make) glorious (things), glory, (very) great, be grievous, harden, be (make) heavy, be heavier, lay heavily, (bring to, come to, do, get, be had in) honour (self), (be) honourable (man), lade, X more be laid, make self many, nobles, prevail, promote (to honour), be rich, be (go) sore, stop.

It is absolutely right that we should respect our fathers and mothers all of our lives, even if or when they act dishonorably. But to blindly follow them is pure folly. We know that the Bible does teach children to obey their parents.

Children, obey your parents in the Lord: for this is right.
EPHESIANS 6:1, KJV

This is good as long as the parents teach them in the Lord. But what if they don't? Look a bit further in Scripture and you can see the admonition to parents.

And, ye fathers, provoke not your children to wrath: but bring them up in the nurture and admonition of the Lord.
EPHESIANS 6:4, KJV

The absence of this verse in the raising of children is the number one cause of rebellion in teenagers and children, causing them to dishonor and to disobey their parents. Plain parents who exercise control over their children by condemning them using the "honour thy father and thy mother" verse have already lost them because they have failed to observe the "do not provoke them to wrath" verse.

If atheist or Islamic parents refuse to let their children become Christians, does that mean that they will go to hell if they do convert to Christianity? Of course not. Neither are your children bound by some law to follow their parents to hell. Nowhere does the Bible teach that it is a sin to leave a church, especially one that teaches strange doctrines. Rather, Scripture teaches that we should not have fellowship with them.

Be ye not unequally yoked together with unbelievers: for what fellowship hath righteousness with unrighteousness? and what communion hath light with darkness?
2 CORINTHIANS 6:14, KJV

Then Peter and the other apostles answered and said, We ought to obey God rather than men.
(ACTS 5:29, KJV)

The Apostle Paul was transformed by the revelation of Jesus Christ after Jesus had ascended into Heaven. He had been a Pharisee of high degree, one who persecuted the Christian church. Yet after he came to Jesus, he forsook his Jewish upbringing to follow Jesus and became a Christian.

> *Circumcised the eighth day, of the stock of Israel, of the tribe of Benjamin, an Hebrew of the Hebrews; as touching the law, a Pharisee; Concerning zeal, persecuting the church; touching the righteousness which is in the law, blameless. But what things were gain to me, those I counted loss for Christ. Yea doubtless, and I count all things but loss for the excellency of the knowledge of Christ Jesus my Lord: for whom I have suffered the loss of all things, and do count them but dung, that I may win Christ,*
> PHILIPPIANS 3:5-8, KJV

As we all know, Paul wrote much of our New Testament. He was greatly persecuted by the Jews and Pharisees, and eventually because of his faith and outspoken witness for the Gosple, he was martyred by the Romans. The fear, intimidation, and condemnation that the Amish and many other plain religions instill into the hearts of their membership is Satanic. All other cult groups use the same kind of fear and intimidation. This keeps people within their grasp, both of the prelates and of Satan. It keeps souls away from the light of Jesus. It is most certainly not some method they find in the Bible. We are to fear God with a sense of awesome fear. We are not to fear man.

> *And I say unto you my friends, Be not afraid of them that kill the body, and after that have no more that they can do. But I will forewarn you whom ye shall fear: Fear him, which after he hath killed hath power to cast into hell; yea, I say unto you, Fear him.*
> LUKE 12:4-5, KJV

Another deceptive method of fear which is projected toward those who want to leave the Amish and seek a true Christian church is the fear of having their children go "out into the world." The Amish have more than enough wild, rebellious youth. They also have unruly married church members. They even have ministers and elders who get into all sorts of drunkenness, drugs, fornication, and adultery, and who are disrespectful and rude.

Unfortunately, some of the children of those who leave the Amish fall prey to the outside world. However, the percentage of children lost to the world among those who leave a plain church for the sake of the Gospel is very small. Compared to those who see the truth but choose to stay Amish, it is small indeed. How can those who remain condemn those who leave when their children depart into the world more than the children of those who leave? Having children in Africa, or China, or Haiti doing missionary work for the Gospel is much different than having one's children go out into the world.

Parents who turn to Jesus for salvation have life giving truth to impart to their children, not harsh rules and strange behaviors.

This myth, like many others which are held among the plain people, is a fable, not the truth. Parents who turn to Jesus for salvation have life giving truth to impart to their children, not harsh rules and strange behaviors. These theories are wrong and people should pay no attention to them at all. They are deceptive and far too many have been deceived.

For there are many unruly and vain talkers and deceivers, specially they of the circumcision.
TITUS 1:10, KJV

We who are born again do not need the law to keep us from sin. Jesus is able to keep us far better than the law, far better than some homemade commandment of men.

> *Not giving heed to Jewish fables, and commandments*
> *of men, that turn from the truth.*
> TITUS 1:14, KJV

> *Wherefore if ye be dead with Christ from the rudiments of the world,*
> *why, as though living in the world, are ye subject to ordinances,*
> *(Touch not; taste not; handle not; Which all are to perish with*
> *the using;) after the commandments and doctrines of men?*
> COLOSSIANS 2:20-22, KJV

> *But if ye be led of the Spirit, ye are not under the law.*
> GALATIANS 5:18, KJV

> *But the fruit of the Spirit is love, joy, peace, longsuffering, gentleness,*
> *goodness, faith, Meekness, temperance: against such there is no law.*
> GALATIANS 5:22-23, KJV

If those who are born again, or even others, decide to leave a church that does not teach the truth, there is no Biblical teaching against it. Actually, there is biblical teaching in favor of leaving such a church.

> *Now I urge you, brethren, note those who cause divisions*
> *and offenses, contrary to the doctrine which you learned,*
> *and avoid them. For those who are such do not serve our*
> *Lord Jesus Christ, but their own belly, and by smooth words*
> *and flattering speech deceive the hearts of the simple.*
> ROMANS 16:17-18, NKJV

We must keep ourselves from this dead religion. They do not teach the truth but pervert the truth to justify their doctrine. These men are evil self serving ministers of death.

> *For such are false apostles, deceitful workers, transforming themselves into apostles of Christ. And no wonder! For Satan himself transforms himself into an angel of light.*
> 2 CORINTHIANS 11:13-14, NKJV

> *… unloving, unforgiving, slanderers, without self-control, brutal, despisers of good, traitors, headstrong, haughty, lovers of pleasure rather than lovers of God, having a form of godliness but denying its power. And from such people turn away!*
> 2 TIMOTHY 3:3-5, NKJV

These ministers of darkness know the scriptures quite well yet they do not understand them for the scriptures are spiritually discerned. They will use all sorts of verses such as:

> *Children obey your parents*
> EPHESIANS 6:1

> *Honour thy father and thy mother.*
> EXODUS 20:12

> *Let every soul be subject to the higher powers.*
> ROMANS 13:1

> *Obey them that have the rule over you and submit yourselves.*
> HEBREWS 13:17

While all of these verses are true, there is one that overrules them all:

> *We ought to obey God rather than men.*
> ACTS 5:29

While we should "obey those who have the rule over us and submit ourselves to them" (Hebrews 13:17), we should never, ever submit ourselves to those who do not preach the truth, to those who are more concerned about our clothes than our souls.

We must choose those to whom we submit ourselves according to God's word, and this decision must not be hindered by false doctrines. Otherwise, we too, will fall into the hands of the enemy. All of the apostles, and those martyred throughout the history of Christianity, were killed because of accusations that they refused to submit to authority, or to accept correction, that they caused divisions, or were disobedient to parents. They would not submit themselves to the church or its bishops, who claimed to be ordained of God to keep them and to watch their souls. But they, like us, knew through the leading of the Holy Ghost that to obey men is death. To obey God is life, even when there are parents and clergymen who try to trip us up with Scripture proofs. Remember, Jesus said His followers would be persecuted.

If you believe you can remain Amish after having been born again, consider these questions. How can you justify being part of a religion that excommunicates repentant sinners and those who are born again? How can you live under a system that forces their doctrines and commandments of men onto born again Christians and excommunicates those who leave the Amish Church? By taking communion with them, you signify that you agree with them and their doctrine as a brother, whether good or bad.

> And Jesus answered and said, Verily I say unto you, There is
> no man that hath left house, or brethren, or sisters, or father,
> or mother, or wife, or children, or lands, for my sake, and the
> gospel's, But he shall receive an hundredfold now in this time,

houses, and brethren, and sisters, and mothers, and children, and lands, with persecutions; and in the world to come eternal life.
MARK 10:29-30, KJV

Understand this and don't be frightened by it. It feels horrible to be rejected, persecuted, and excommunicated, and shunned by people you love. Don't think of it that way. Rather, count it all joy that you have been counted worthy to suffer with the Lord Jesus Christ for the sake of the Gospel.

Blessed are ye, when men shall hate you, and when they shall separate you from their company, and shall reproach you, and cast out your name as evil, for the Son of man's sake. Rejoice ye in that day, and leap for joy: for, behold, your reward is great in heaven: for in the like manner did their fathers unto the prophets.
LUKE 6:22-23, KJV

The Apostle Paul said;"Yea, and all that will live godly in Christ Jesus shall suffer persecution"
2 TIMOTHY 3:12, KJV

And they departed from the presence of the council, rejoicing that they were counted worthy to suffer shame for His name.
ACTS 5:41, KJV

Which is a manifest token of the righteous judgment of God, that ye may be counted worthy of the kingdom of God, for which ye also suffer:
2 THESSALONIANS 1:5, KJV

14

Chapter Fourteen

THE FUN CHURCH

I t should be obvious why there is so little persecution of Christians
in America. Don't misunderstand me. No one wants to suffer—not
for any reason. Religious persecution is no exception. As Christians, we
should not cause riots or disturbances with the motive of being ridiculed
or scorned, just to say we have suffered persecution. If we act in an
arrogant manner and evangelize by being pushy and forceful with the
Gospel, we will be scoffed at and mocked and people will hate us. But
that would not be suffering persecution for the sake of the Gospel. That
would only be getting what we deserve. (See 2 Peter 2:20)

Unfortunately, the greatest part of the American church has been lulled
to sleep. They are comfortable in a setting of religious freedom. Indeed,
there is much money that can be made in religion. Church houses have
gone from secluded caves to multimillion dollar castles. How can it be
possible that anyone cannot see through this, even someone who merely
professes to be Christian and is utterly lukewarm?

Jesus himself gave the parable of the rich man and Lazarus, a story
that points out the inconsistencies that are so apparent in the churches of

today. (See Luke 16:19-31). Think of all the good those billions of dollars could do for the poor people in the third world countries of the world. The Lord said—

> *I know thy works, that thou art neither cold nor hot: I would*
> *thou wert cold or hot. So then because thou art lukewarm,*
> *and neither cold nor hot, I will spue thee out of my mouth.*
> REVELATION 3:15-16, KJV

What a joke these plush churches have become. Their preachers have to go through a seminary to learn how to preach and how captivate the attention of an audience. They have no idea who the Holy Spirit is. Many of their messages seem to be focused on "hyper-grace." Messages on repentance are cast aside as "judgmental" or "legalistic." Churches have become activity centers which meet just enough to justify all the fun they are having. They want to make everyone feel good about themselves and the lives they live. The preachers preach for money, and the more they can justify everyone's sins, the more money they will get paid. So many things of the world, divorce and remarriage, homosexuality, fornication and adultery, big vacations, fancy houses and cars, and sports, have all found their way into the church. Preachers want their money as well, and they know that if they preach against these things, they will lose a lot of the money that is tossed in offering plates once or twice a week.

Do you remember reading in the beginning of this book the phrase *panem et circenses*. It means bread and circus, a phrase that was applied as the only needs of the pagans at the time of the early churches. Today's modern churches are no different, except that they have also become lukewarm.

A preacher of a large congregation once got a clear revelation from the Lord and began to preach the truth. One Sunday morning while preaching, he told his congregation, "You are not going to hell for watching football on Sunday night rather than coming to church." Imagine the smiles, nods, and sighs of relief that brought. But then after a slight pause he said "but you are doing it because you are already going to hell!" Imagine that response. He lost about eighty percent of his membership. Praise the Lord! That is called "house cleaning" in a church. Get rid of all the lukewarmness. The focus should not be on the quantity but the quality of Christians attending the church.

Why do people attend in the first place? Are they coming to hear some more of those conscience soothing, ear tickling sermons that roll off of the well-practiced, yet forked-tongue of some divorced, seminary taught, plush preacher? Or is it because they are gathered in sacred awe of their Lord and Master Jesus Christ? Is it because they are gathered in the assembly of the saints with other like minded, "on fire for God" believers? Will they listen to a minister who has no formal education from any earthly schoolmaster? Will they hear the one who,

... the assembly of the saints with other like minded, "on fire for God"...

by his much seeking of God through fasting and prayer, has received God's word in his heart? Do they understand that he is willing to share that message, even though he receives not one cent for his efforts and has a day job just like the rest of the congregation.

A sermon is not dependant on how much time we spend trying to make it. It depends on how much time we spend in holy devotion before God that makes the sermon have power. Preachers who preach according to their own efforts preach death. They often end up not living according to their own sermons, or they make excuses for sin in order not to prick their own consciences. They will teach that Jesus died for all your sins, but because no one is perfect it is alright to "slip up and fall" into an occasional sin. They will let people believe it is okay to sin occasionally, as long as they are still trying to be good. But that's a lie. Jesus gave us a full victory over sin, not a partial one.

> *Whosoever is born of God doth not commit sin; for his seed*
> *remaineth in him: and he cannot sin, because he is born of God.*
> 1 JOHN 3:9, KJV

This verse should not be controversial, but it usually disturbs those who have never truly come to Jesus for cleansing from all sin. Indeed, we are all sinners because we have all sinned. But to continue in willful sin, or even repeated sin, is where a line must be drawn.

> *For if we sin willfully after that we have received the knowledge*
> *of the truth, there remaineth no more sacrifice for sins*
> HEBREWS 10:26, KJV

Yet these ministers will never go confront sin in this way, because to them it seems impossible to maintain a godly membership. It probably would be difficult to preach a sermon like this and not turn away eighty percent of the membership. So they compromise with the truth and continue in their ministry of death. They make church a a "fun place to go," a place where there are many fun functions to enjoy to keep everyone on a high and light note. They play silly little cartoons of old Godly prophets and of Jesus for all the little children. They preach high spirited, light, even funny sermons for the adults. After all, God is a kind God isn't he? They teach that such a kind God would never cast the people He created into an eternal hell. But hell is real.

*And death and hell were cast into the lake of fire. This is
the second death. And whosoever was not found written
in the book of life was cast into the lake of fire.*
REVELATION 20:14-15, KJV

Lukewarm Christians, and those who teach false doctrine and the commandments of men, need to get a small glimpse of the awfulness of hell. Then they would not waste their time having fun time at church. Neither would they waste their time telling men how they must dress or keep their beard. The legalistic, plain church and the loose-living "fun" church are equally deceived. They both present a message that leads to spiritual death, a message either without hope or one with totally false hope.

*And the devil that deceived them was cast into the lake of
fire and brimstone, where the beast and the false prophet are,
and shall be tormented day and night forever and ever.*
REVELATION 20:10, KJV

They are no better or worse than each other. The Bible makes no distinction between the two, but calls them both false prophets. We Christians do not have the time to have many pleasures, nor do we have the time to dictate to others with our self righteous doctrine. But not many are found in the category of those who suffer persecution.

*Yea, and all that will live godly in Christ
Jesus shall suffer persecution.*
2 TIMOTHY 3:12, KJV

They have traded their rocks and rotten tomatoes for money and fame. They have traded "standing on an upside down bucket on a dirty street corner, preaching to lost and desperate sinners" for plush, air conditioned pulpits. There they can preach to a sleeping crowd that could not care less, as long as they can continue in sin and still offer them hope. They have traded the truth of the Gospel for the commandments of men, and the leadership of the Holy Spirit for the dictatorship of man. The Bible says—

> *Blessed are ye, when men shall hate you, and when they shall*
> *separate you from their company, and shall reproach you,*
> *and cast out your name as evil, for the Son of man's sake.*
> LUKE 6:22, KJV

> *Woe unto you, when all men shall speak well of you!*
> *For so did their fathers to the false prophets.*
> LUKE 6:26, KJV

> *Go to now, ye rich men, weep and howl for*
> *your miseries that shall come upon you.*
> JAMES 5:1, KJV

Because of all their trading with the devil, the prelates have interpreted Luke 6:22 as a command to excommunicate those who disagree with them. They preach that you will go to hell if you are excommunicated for your faith in Jesus. The other group interprets Luke 6:26 as "you need a bunch of buddies to play golf with." Of course, they believe it's okay to be involved in sports as long as you can attach it to some sort of church event. Furthermore, it doesn't do to have anyone get mad at you if you present them with the truth. So it is best to remain silent about Jesus.

James 5:1 seems to be interpreted by them in this manner. "If you keep all the commandments of the church and stay in the *ordnung*, God will make you rich." Can you sense the irony here? The churches which should be directing people toward heaven are paving the way to hell, either by harsh rules or by ignoring holy living.

WOE TO YOU ELDERS WHO DENY THE TRUTH!

But woe to you, Scribes and Pharisees, hypocrites! For you shut up the kingdom of heaven against men; for you neither go in yourselves, nor do you allow those who are entering to go in.
MATTHEW 23:13, NKJV

Chapter Fifteen

THE CHURCH WITH NO RULES

Those who say a church cannot operate without rules are absolutely right. However, those who believe a church must function with man developed rules—*ordnung*, standards, or at the very least, some brotherly agreements—are fooling themselves. They should ordain a preacher who is willing to preach the true Gospel for what it is, not for some set of man-made rules.

We are not our own masters, no matter how hard we try to be. So, to say that we will not be ruled might well be saying we will be our own masters. The Holy Spirit is totally capable of doing His work without our help. But a church that does not acknowledge that the leadership of the Holy Spirit it totally sufficient will be bound to man-made laws. Ultimately, we all serve God, or else we will serve the devil.

The law was given to the Jews in the wilderness at Mt. Sinai. The Bible teaches us that it was ordained by the Angels.

Wherefore then serveth the law? It was added because of transgressions, till the seed should come to whom the promise was made; and it was ordained by angels in the hand of a mediator.
GALATIANS 3:19, KJV

This seed refers to the generational seed of Abraham—Jesus. This was the first covenant. But after Jesus died and rose from the grave, we live under a new covenant. The Old Testament stops with Jesus and the New Covenant, the New Testament begins with Him.

For if that first covenant had been faultless, then should no place have been sought for the second. For finding fault with them, He saith, Behold, the days come, saith the Lord, when I will make a new covenant with the house of Israel and with the house of Judah. Not according to the covenant that I made with their fathers in the day when I took them by the hand to lead them out of the land of Egypt; because they continued not in my covenant, and I regarded them not, saith the Lord.

For this is the covenant that I will make with the house of Israel after those days, saith the Lord; I will put my laws into their mind, and write them in their hearts: and I will be to them a God, and they shall be to me a people: And they shall not teach every man his neighbour, and every man his brother, saying, Know the Lord: for all shall know me, from the least to the greatest.
HEBREWS 8:7-11, KJV

This passage, of itself, should settle any argument, but it will not. In fact, the entire Bible does not change those who do not want to see. These verses in Hebrews 8:7-11 clearly state that. God's Word is saying that there was fault found in the first covenant (v. 7). God makes no mistakes, nor has He ever. So, if the first law was found to be imperfect, it is certain that no Amish, or any other religion, will ever come up with one that is. Perhaps they believe they have discovered some divine law that God forgot to add, some rule that makes their version so much greater than His. Perhaps their law is so divine that they now have the right to excommunicate those who disobey it?

In verse 8, God acknowledges that He found fault in them, not the law He gave, but in the people who could not and would not live up to it. Thus, He was going to make a new one, (verse 9) not according to the one He made with the Israelites when He led them out of slavery. But, (verse 10) of this new covenant, He said, "I will put my laws into their minds and write them on their hearts."

We are all given a living conscience. If we allow it to work and respond to it, we can be led in all righteousness through the power of the Holy Spirit. This is why we do not need anyone to tell us how to dress, or whether we should wear a beard, or drive a car. Cars do not cause us to sin, refusing to subject our consciences to the leadership of the Holy Spirit does.

> *We are all given a living conscience. If we allow it to work and respond to it, we can be led in all righteousness through the power of the Holy Spirit.*

In verse 11, He is saying that we will not need man to teach us how to serve the Lord. "for all shall know" (meaning all Christians). Those who serve Him in all truth, who have no man made church rules or *ordnung*, but who are guided through the power of the Holy Spirit, shall know. Those who love their brothers, who have the fruits of righteousness, and are abiding in the law of Christ—they shall know.

Of course Satan will not stand for this idea of having us be free from bondage. He will do everything in his power to transfer the reins of power from the Holy Spirit back to some man whom he can control. Then as time goes by, in his cunning subtle ways, he will tear them further and further away from God. Through men's rules, he will inject his own cunningly devised fables into the church, fables that look like righteousness.

> *Now therefore why tempt ye God, to put a yoke upon the*
> *neck of the disciples, which neither our fathers nor we were*
> *able to bear? But we believe that through the grace of the*
> *Lord Jesus Christ we shall be saved, even as they.*
> ACTS 15:10-11, KJV

Essentially, if a church operates by its own standards and rejects the leadership of the Holy Spirit, it has become lawless—"workers of iniquity."

> *And then will I profess unto them, I never knew*
> *you: depart from me, ye that work iniquity.*
> MATTHEW 7:23, KJV

The Mafia, pirate ships, bands of robbers, and guerrilla bands all have some form of law. Of course, none of these are in the Bible. Are they righteous? Just because a particular group has rules does not mean that group is righteous. Neither does it mean their rules are righteous. Righteousness is not defined by man's ideas but by the truth of the Bible. It is good that the Amish do not rob and steal. But that does not make them better than other groups. The Bible gives no more hope to false prophets than it does to more obvious sinners, like robbers and murderers.

So many of the church's rules look righteous, when in reality, they are not. They are just cunningly devised fables. They condemn people who have committed no sin. What would happen if an Amish man drove a car to help a friend in real trouble, like being pinned down under a piece of farm equipment? What if he saved his friend's life? He would very likely be excommunicated and handed over to Satan for destruction of his flesh because he drove a car. The preachers who would excommunicate him might well be guilty of adultery, or drunkenness, or witchcraft. Yet, rules are rules. This man who saved his friend's life would have done a Godly deed. He committed no sin in God's eyes or his own. Yet, when he broke a man made rule, he was condemned.

Satan is the author of deception and of confusion—the father of all lies. He is the author of the rules which make the Bible seem confusing. These rules do not include the ones we have in our homes for our own little children. We parents are admonished to raise our children for the Lord, and this requires us to make reasonable rules.

> *Train up a child in the way he should go: and*
> *when he is old, he will not depart from it.*
> PROVERBS 22:6, KJV

The law is to be kept in place for those who are not born again.

> *But we know that the law is good, if a man use it lawfully; Knowing*
> *this, that the law is not made for a righteous man, but for the*
> *lawless and disobedient, for the ungodly and for sinners, for unholy*
> *and profane, for murderers of fathers and murderers of mothers,*
> *for manslayers, For whoremongers, for them that defile themselves*
> *with mankind, for menstealers, for liars, for perjured persons, and*
> *if there be any other thing that is contrary to sound doctrine;*
> 1 TIMOTHY 1:8-10, KJV

Wherefore the law was our schoolmaster to bring us unto
Christ, that we might be justified by faith. But after that
faith is come, we are no longer under a schoolmaster.
GALATIANS 3:24-25, KJV

Satan desperately desires to keep us under the law in order to deprive us of the fullness of the grace of God. He desires to keep us from that very life that defeated him when Christ rose from the grave.

For as many as are of the works of the law are under the curse:
for it is written, Cursed is every one that continueth not in all
things which are written in the book of the law to do them.
GALATIANS 3:10, KJV

Jesus redeemed us from this curse of the law, Christ hath
redeemed us from the curse of the law, being made a curse for us:
for it is written, Cursed is every one that hangeth on a tree.
GALATIANS 3:13, KJV

Why would anyone desire to return to the law to become righteous, especially when they know that is impossible?

If we have been born again and continue trying to live in righteousness through the law and cause others to do so as well we have become like the proverb:

But it is happened unto them according to the true proverb,
The dog is turned to his own vomit again; and the sow
that was washed to her wallowing in the mire.
2 PETER 2:22, KJV

Jesus, after He rose from the dead, spent a short time on earth with His disciples. He became a living testimony that He was victorious over death and hell. He proved that He had become victorious over Satan. He became the New Testament, a new covenant, unlike the old one (see Hebrews 9). While Jesus was here on earth, the Holy Spirit was not yet given freely to all men. Only by being in the physical presence of Jesus Christ could anyone be in the presence of the living God.

If the Holy Spirit had been given then, people would have spent less time following Jesus. Without a doubt, His mission would have been less effective. Perhaps He would have not been crucified as He was. If the Holy Spirit had been available before Jesus ascended to the Father, the High priests might have understood that "truly, this was the Son of God." That would have prevented Him from being crucified for the remission of sins. But Jesus said—

> *"Nevertheless I tell you the truth. It is to your advantage that I go away; for if I do not go away, the Helper will not come to you; but if I depart, I will send Him to you. "And when He has come, He will convict the world of sin, and of righteousness, and of judgment: "of sin, because they do not believe in Me; "of righteousness, because I go to My Father and you see Me no more; "of judgment, because the ruler of this world is judged. "I still have many things to say to you, but you cannot bear them now. "However, when He, the Spirit of truth, has come, He will guide you into all truth; for He will not speak on His own authority, but whatever He hears He will speak; and He will tell you things to come."He will glorify Me, for He will take of what is Mine and declare it to you.*
> JOHN 16:7-14, NKJV

This great promise makes it very difficult to prove or justify any man made, or church ordained, commandments or rules of men using the New Testament Bible. Notice those religions which enforce their ideas, their brotherly agreements, their rules or *ordnung*. More often than not they have only a vague recollection of the Holy Spirit. Maybe they have none at all. If they do acknowledge Him, it will be dimly, and certainly not as the Divine Messenger or Leader. They do not see Him as One who would be able to unfailingly lead them into a Godly Christian walk in life. These religions who insist in their church rules do so only because they do not know Jesus in a real way. Neither are they led by the Holy Ghost, as Jesus promised us.

Anyone can become a preacher of rules, twisting certain Scripture references into his sermon to justify it as righteous. But it takes a true man of God to become any kind of Godly minister or bishop. A truly born again Christian would only want, or even be right in submitting himself to a Godly minister.

> *Obey those who rule over you, and be submissive, for they watch*
> *out for your souls, as those who must give account. Let them do so*
> *with joy and not with grief, for that would be unprofitable for you.*
> HEBREWS 13:17, NKJV

We should not be part of a church that is more concerned with our clothes, our facial hair, or what we drive, than the status of our souls. It is time to submit ourselves to a more qualified authority, for we are not to be unequally joined with those who are not truly Christians.

> *Be ye not unequally yoked together with unbelievers: for*
> *what fellowship hath righteousness with unrighteousness?*
> *and what communion hath light with darkness?*
> 2 CORINTHIANS 6:14, KJV

It is not sin to leave a church or religion for the sake of righteousness. Nowhere does the Bible teach us that it is. Causing strife, enmity, and division is sin, but leaving a church is not divisive. It is more like something Paul and the other apostles would have done to abandon an unrighteous religion. That is actually what they did when they left the Jewish churches.

*Now I beseech you, brethren, mark them which
cause divisions and offences contrary to the doctrine
which ye have learned; and avoid them.*
ROMANS 16:17, KJV

Causing divisions is what these plain or orthodox religions are doing in the Church of Christ. They lure or keep members away from the true Church by their intimidating and evil tactics. Only a true God-fearing, born again, Holy Spirit filled man is able to minister to people as Jesus commanded. He will plant a Godly seed, water and nurture it into fruit bearing Christianity that is pleasing to God. Ministers need to preach a clear unobstructed, Gospel message, holding nothing back. It should be received through much prayer and time spent seeking the Lord. If they will do their part and preach a true message, God will do the rest. He will write His laws upon their hearts and into their minds (See Hebrews 8:10). He will convict people concerning what they should wear, how and if a beard should be worn, and whether or not a man should wear a hat to church or at work.

Ministers need to preach a clear unobstructed, Gospel message, holding nothing back.

If a preacher is bound by church rules and regulations, he must watch what he says. He is not in any way, shape, or form able to follow God's call in a pure unhindered way. He must to preach life. The only alternative is to preach death. We cannot preach both life and death. We cannot preach life if we must please man or man's rules. It is impossible to serve God and man when it comes to preaching God's word, because God's Word does not please all men. God's Word does not even please many preachers and bishops who are ordained, even though God was not consulted about their ordination.

Who changed the truth of God into a lie, and worshipped and served the creature more than the Creator, who is blessed forever. Amen.
ROMANS 1:25, KJV

Serving the creature more than the Creator includes man as well as beasts. It extends out to the fear of man or the love of man, more than the fear or love of God. Yet, the fear of man has entered the hearts of many preachers. They are afraid to speak up for the truth. They are afraid they too will become excommunicated if they do not preach from a pre-assigned text. These premeditated, pre-assigned texts have been handed down over generations so that nothing that contradicts the traditional teachings of the forefathers will be spoken. This is the same reason Jesus condemned the Pharisees.

And He said unto them, Full well ye reject the commandment of God, that ye may keep your own tradition.
MARK 7:9, KJV

It is a very serious offense to reject the commandment of God. We should never be part of any church or religious group that practices this, especially if they excommunicate those who leave them because of their false teachings. The *Martyrs Mirror* (page 364 article 11) teaches that—

"The excommunications and ecclesiastical punishments decreed by the prelates, we are not to regard. They too, faced persecutions from families and churches for their beliefs, and also read the same Bible that we do."

If you are reproached for the name of Christ, blessed are you,
for the spirit of glory and of God rests upon you. On their
part He is blasphemed, but on your part He is glorified.
1 PETER 4:14 NKJV

No religion is exempt from the teachings of the Bible, no matter what reasons they offer. As mentioned before, the law is good only to bring us to Christ. It is not sufficient for our salvation. Neither will it ever make us righteous enough for the Kingdom of God. Under the law, we fall into sin time after time because there is no power over our spirits to keep us from sin. The transformation that comes as part of the born again experience is the only way we will ever overcome the temptation to sin. Temptation is the root of evil from which sin originates. (See James 1:13-14. It is only through the eradication of this temptation that we will ever be free from sin.

This is what it means to be born again. You must be transformed by the blood of the Lamb into a new creature, one who thinks differently as well as one who behaves differently. For someone who is living this new life, the law, whether it is the law of Moses, or some cheap man made version, will not do any good. Only the Holy Spirit will be able to keep us from sin. Jesus said: *"God is a Spirit: and they that worship Him must worship Him in spirit and in truth"* (John 4:24, KJV).

The Apostle Paul clearly taught against law for born again believers.

But if ye be led of the Spirit, ye are not under the law.
GALATIANS 5:18, KJV

As Christians, we are taught to love one another and to be kind towards one another.

> *This is my commandment, That ye love one*
> *another, as I have loved you.*
> JOHN 15:12, KJV

> *Bear ye one another's burdens, and so fulfil the law of Christ.*
> GALATIANS 6:2, KJV

All the rules these religions make to help them keep the commandments of Jesus Christ are like all the rules the Pharisees made. They are to help them keep the laws of God, but they don't. In fact, Jesus condemned them for their man made version of righteousness. If no justification is found in a law ordained of angels and given by God, how will righteousness come from one that is ordained and dictated by mere man?

> *Knowing that a man is not justified by the works of the law, but by*
> *the faith of Jesus Christ, even we have believed in Jesus Christ, that*
> *we might be justified by the faith of Christ, and not by the works*
> *of the law: for by the works of the law shall no flesh be justified.*
> GALATIANS 2:16, KJV

The Amish bishops and ministers have set themselves up as gods, holding their own traditional laws higher than the doctrines of the Holy Bible. Of course they will deny it, but many of them realize it is neither biblical nor right to excommunicate people for their faith or for repenting of their sins. Yet, because of their fear of man, they continue to go along with it. This is what Jesus meant when He confronted the Pharisees.

> *And He said unto them, Full well ye reject the commandment*
> *of God, that ye may keep your own tradition.*
> MARK 7:9, KJV

The law said "Thou shalt not commit adultery" (Exodus 20:14, KJV), Jesus said—

> *But I say unto you, That whosoever looketh on a woman to lust*
> *after her hath committed adultery with her already in his heart.*
> MATTHEW 5:28, KJV

This is only one example of the difference between the Old and New Testaments or covenants. The old was law and good works. The new takes it further, so high, that it cannot possibly be accomplished through the works of the law. Only through rebirth and the power and leadership of the Holy Spirit will we ever arrive at the righteousness that is in Jesus Christ. That, we must achieve in order to reach heaven. Just think about it. You can have more than victory over sin. You can have victory over the lust for sin as well! This is impossible through the law. It is only possible through the saving grace of Jesus Christ as we subject our lives to Jesus. He is the One who has redeemed us from sin. With His own blood, He has ransomed us from Satan and eternal death with the devil and his angels.

There is no power over temptation in the law. Only through the blood of Jesus will we ever reach that high standard of excellence. Only in this will we be able to love and find the peace, the joy, and the assurance of salvation that God has given in Christ Jesus.

> *He has delivered us from the power of darkness and conveyed*
> *us into the kingdom of the Son of His love, in who we have*
> *the redemption through His blood, the forgiveness of sins.*
> COLOSSIANS 1:13-14

16

Chapter Sixteen

LANGUAGES OF DEATH

Arabic is not the dominant language of most of the Islamic countries around the world. Yet the Qur'an, which is the Islamic scripture, is written completely in this language. It is understood in large part by well taught Mullahs—teachers and doctors of Islamic law. Few of the Islamic followers or common Muslims are competent enough in this unpopular and antiquated language. They cannot understand enough of the Qur'an to be able to discern right from wrong concerning Islamic beliefs.

Many of the Muslims one meets on the streets of America will tell you theirs is a beautiful religion, one that ministers love and peace. But this is not true. Their religion promotes jihad (holy war). They teach that those who become martyrs for that faith (like suicide bombers and militants killed in combat) will be highly blessed in heaven. Men believe they will be given as many as seventy virgin girls as part of their reward in heaven. Some teach that young girls should be physically mutilated, something they call female circumcision by which the clitoris of a girl's female genitalia is cut or removed. And these are but three of the evil teachings of Islam.

A man—Muhammad—known throughout Islam as the "prophet," wrote the Qur'an. It is supposedly based on a revelation he received from Allah (the Arabic word for God). Yet, for the first seven years of his revelation, he was unable to convert people to his beliefs. Only his brother-in-law and his wife stood with him.

After seven years, he relocated to another part of the country. There he used brutal and violent methods to force his doctrine onto the poor natives, who submitted out of fear. His promotional methods included many of the same tactics still used today by the Islamic terrorists. Murder, rape, and pillaging, cutting off of fingers, hands, and even arms and legs were methods of interrogation used by Muhammad and his evil followers to instill fear in the hearts of those they were determined to convert. People followed, not because they believed in him or his message of terror, but out of fear. Today, for a Muslim to convert to Christianity is an instant death sentence.

For Muslims, like the Amish, to leave the faith is met with strict shunning and being condemned to hell forever unless one repents.

The Muslims, like the Amish, teach their children and their membership that to leave the faith is met with strict shunning and being condemned to hell forever unless one repents. The Muslims do not allow Christians to promote their faith in Islamic countries. So, many Muslims do not comprehend the full extent of the darkness their religion holds. They are not told, and many cannot read for themselves because they are deprived of education. Moreover, the Qur'an (Koran) may only be read in Arabic if they are to be truly Muslim. The Mullahs in America, and even in other countries, will not teach all of the Qur'an.

They do not want their followers to know the truth about their evil doctrine.

The Roman Catholic churches used Latin for centuries. It was the language of ancient Rome, but today it is a dead language. No one speaks it apart from the Catholic Church. Even here in the United States, it was used until recent years. Very few people apart from the clergy understand Latin. So here too is a church that promotes false religion in a vague and dark way. Yet, it is not obviously dark enough to raise questions from the average lay member. If no one understands Latin how can anyone be spiritually enlightened through their services and masses? The truth is that no one really is, at least not in a spiritual way.

Of course they may go away inspired or feeling emotionally strengthened. But what inspired them? Was it the great vaulted cathedrals, the flickering candles, the chanted songs and prayers, and the symbolic ritualistic form of worship?

The Amish also use an obscure language—a dialect of German that is no longer in use anywhere else in the world. So, for them it has become the perfect language to hide behind. Very few of them realize they use this language by influence of the devil to hide the demonic darkness behind all of their religious rituals and teachings. If they do, they don't admit it. Very few of the lay membership understand much of the German used in church services. All the Bible reading, songs, and prayers are in this German dialect. As for sermons, preachers use as much of this language as possible when they preach their messages. The more a preacher can use it, the more highly respected he will be among others of the clergymen and elders.

Using too many English words can result in trouble for a preacher. He might even be silenced and disallowed to preach. Were it not for the "Amish" or "Dutch" dialect (their native language) mixed in with the rest of a sermon, most people would understand absolutely nothing. Sermons, songs, and especially the prayers are delivered in old German. Prayers are recited from prayer books (very old ones, of course) and these are usually given in a fast, high pitched, sing-song chant. This chanting style of prayer has been popular throughout history by nearly all of the pagan god worshipers, including the Native Americans, the Baal worshipers, and the worshippers of Molech (the god to which children were sacrificed, offered alive as a burnt offering).

In some of the more conservative Amish Churches, those which are even more plain in their lifestyle, it is not allowed anymore. It is banned by the prelates. This language is not taught in their partial schools anymore. This prevents children from becoming wiser than their parents or the bishops and preachers of the church. They fear the children will begin to understand their sermons and compare them to the true written word of God. They do not want the children to question the teachings of the church for fear they will leave it altogether.

Some preachers will encourage their congregations not to teach the children much from the Bible, in order to keep them in innocence. They believe that innocence, or rather ignorance, helps to protect them from facing too much accountability on the day of judgment. Their most effective means of control is an ignorant soul, one that fears hell, follows man, and lives by their rules. How demonic and contrary to Bible teachings this is.

The Amish also place great emphasis on emotions and signs to justify their religion. If an Amish preacher can stir his congregation into a tearful, emotional state, he then has them convinced of whatever he wishes them to believe. They also place great emphasis on the experiences of the dying to gauge their walk in life. If an Amish man is dying and sees heaven. it is considered to be an omen. If others follow him and live as he did, they believe they will surely make it into heaven. But Jesus never taught that. He said:

> *And these signs shall follow them that believe; In my name shall*
> *they cast out devils; they shall speak with new tongues; They shall*
> *take up serpents; and if they drink any deadly thing, it shall not*
> *hurt them; they shall lay hands on the sick, and they shall recover.*
> MARK 16:17-18 KJV

Nothing in the Bible indicates that to have a revelation of heaven at death is to be saved. We will all go to hell if we follow men and their ideas. Jesus said:

> *...I am the way, the truth, and the life: no man*
> *cometh unto the Father, but by me.*
> JOHN 14:6, KJV

Do not be deceived, no vision, dream, or language can change the authenticity of God's word.

Chapter Seventeen

A GODLY SEED???

Why do so many youths, especially among the plain religions, act the way they do? They act far worse than their "worldly" counterparts—drinking, using drugs, and falling into fornication. They are disrespectful and arrogant and usually quite loud in their behavior, especially around other youths. Yet, many parents feel it is much safer for their children to be hounding around like this, testing the ways of the world than to attend a revival meeting where they might get born again. If they were to find the true Jesus and be saved, they would be cast aside from the Amish and the family would be dissolved.

Rumspringa they call it. It is supposedly a time for deciding whether or not to join the Amish Church. But the word means running around, and that can be a very wild and rebellious time. If one could comprehend, even a little bit, the twisted dark thinking that allows this, it might change. But this is far from a form of godly religion. Yet, it is assumed that youth will go through a season of running around. After that period of time, they will settle down and become submissive to the church and its prelates.

Actually, attending a Gospel service or a revival meeting might result in some youths leaving the Amish Church for a more spiritual one. So, giving in to a period of sinful pursuit is tolerated. But the end results can be tragic. They can lead to wrecked homes, bad marriages, drinking, drug abuse, continued fornication and even adultery. Many plain youth and young fathers have sought relief from their guilt and the burden sin they carry, but they have found none. Because of the rules, they are convinced that if they bring their burden to the church, the only relief will be public exposure. Almost always, they must go to the bishop and confess. This forces a public confession, usually accompanied by excommunication, depending on the severity of the offense. Even an individual's level of social influence can have a significant impact on the severity of a decreed punishment.

However, no sin will ever be forgiven because of this, not a single one. Forgiveness does not come from punishment. It comes from God. These imposed humiliations cause many people to fall into depression. In their hearts, they still seek freedom from their burdens. Many strong young men have ended up becoming addicted to alcohol and mind altering drugs when the real answer to their need would have been Jesus.

This is another one of Satan's cunningly devised fables, a continuation of modern day witchcraft. Medication is not the answer for these people. They will never be healed by taking more and more drugs. If the medicine actually healed the problem, this would be altogether different. But it's not. It is so obviously witchcraft (*pharmakia*) because it is a way to control people's minds. Yet, their problems are never brought out and dealt with. This dead religion and the way they deal with their problems is such a masterpieces of Satan's dark deception.

It all begins as a plain, outwardly good looking religion. Children are raised in a religious atmosphere. But from the church, they understand very little from the three hours they sit on hard, backless wooden benches. At nine years of age, children no longer sit with their parents. They spend Sunday mornings with other boys and girls between the ages of nine and sixteen, completely unsupervised by any responsible adults. At the age of sixteen they become youth and begin to run around with others their age.

Sunday afternoons are spent at a gathering where they engage in sports, such as baseball and volleyball. In the winter time, they play games like ping pong, Rook®, or other card games, like poker, hoss, and seven and a half. Many of these card games are gambling games, played for real money. Games like "seven and a half" involve serious amounts of cash where the "pot" might reach hundreds or even thousands of dollars in a single round.

Sunday evenings are often reserved for "singings," events where the youth gather inside a building, usually a barn. There they sing German and English hymns, fellowship with other youth, and have a snack before they return to their homes for the night. Often, the gambling games are carried over to the singing times and continued. Unfortunately, in many communities these gatherings turn out to be something quite different than innocent times of fellowship. They become loud, drunken, drug-riddled parties, with heavy metal, hard rock music, driven through portable CD players. Sometimes, the parties continue deep into the night into the wee hours of the next morning. Dating boys and girls often leave to get by themselves in totally unsupervised circumstances.

Parents, believing their children are being raised in a godly home will entrust them to each other. They also trust them to the spirits that abound in the late night party life. Then, they are surprised and devastated when their children end up in fornication, get arrested for illegal substances, or become pregnant. These same youths, in order to be married, must become members of the church first. That seems not to be a bad idea, but it has no power of salvation. The bad idea lies in the deception imposed upon them, that rebirth is theirs through baptism.

Every two years a church district will offer instruction classes for baptism. Instruction classes involve meeting with the ministers for approximately a half hour every other Sunday morning. What is taught are the eighteen articles of faith of the Amish Church. These are all taught in German. Only a very small number of students understand enough of the instructions to be able to repeat them, even five minutes later.

Before a district announces instructions for baptism, the youth party their lives away. Then, throughout the summer they will settle down. They'll make a few changes to their clothing and hair. They'll take instruction at the bi-weekly church services for the summer. Then they will be baptized and become members of the Amish Church. Baptism requires no testimony to be given, only the affirmation of an oath of allegiance to the Amish Church. What matters is the way their clothes, their hat, their hair, and their other outward appearances look. With baptism accomplished, they are told their sins are now washed away. They will walk away from the church service and the baptism ceremony, supposedly washed clean and free from sin.

This surely sounds convincing, and the feeling of being washed by baptism must feel good. But it lasts only a short time. Sooner or later some of these youth hit a hard time in their life and sink to rock bottom. They don't know where to turn. They have been "baptized" but they are not born again. They have no idea who the Holy Spirit is and have no contact with Him. Temptations rise within. They are under the deception that their baptism cleansed them, so there is nothing else that can be done. They become guilt ridden and have no real peace. Their sins, even the ones committed before they were baptized, come back to haunt them. They could repent to the preachers, but even then excommunication looms large, so they don't. Instead, they backslide into an even murkier depression. Dark sinful thoughts are often accompanied by sinful deeds, and they are faced with a more sinful life than before. They not only are without power over sin and temptation, they are also overwhelmed with serious guilt and self-condemnation

This is a very typical life of an Amish boy. He grows up religious, but the real Jesus is totally absent from his life. He learns sin because he is born in sin, his father was born in sin, and his grandfather was as well. Sin is traceable all the way back to his beginning, but without being born again, that sin cannot be taken away. Some unknown Jesus has been preached to him and his ancestors, and they say they are born again and baptized. But they quickly change the subject. Talking about Jesus is one of the most hated subjects among most Amish men. To them Jesus is vague, a shadowy person from Bible days far removed from today, and talking of Him is something to be ashamed of.

Talking about Jesus is one of the most hated subjects among most Amish men.

This is not only true for Amish. Many religious people do not and cannot relate to a living Jesus. It is why so many of these men and women end up in counseling centers or on mind altering drugs. These offer no hope of ever being free, and sometimes the side effects are even suicidal. They become just another cog on the endless wheel of a dark, dead religion, all engineered by Satan. It keeps men away from the light of Jesus. It gives them medicines that calm the flesh and make them look normal to those who judge by outward appearance and actions. But their souls are left to die, trapped inside medically subdued bodies, dimmed by the dark demonic powers of witchcraft.

Imagine what they could be delivered from if they could go to a church where people are allowed to be free. What would they experience if they went where Jesus is honestly portrayed by a true man of God? What would happen if they heard messages that do not leave out certain parts of the Bible if they don't suit the preacher or his lifestyle? A minister who is not bound by dead religion or the commandments of men can be free to preach the whole Bible. A minister who preaches from the entire Bible can more readily follow the Holy Spirit. He should not be restricted to preaching from pre-assigned texts. He should not be bound to only about 40 of the 260 chapters in the New Testament. Furthermore, he should not be forced to preach in a language people cannot clearly understand.

When depressed people hear the true Gospel, they soon get born again. What could be wrong with that?

Jesus answered and said unto him, Verily, verily, I say unto thee, Except a man be born again, he cannot see the kingdom of God.
JOHN 3:3, KJV

Instead of being depressed, these born again men and women would be more than excited to talk about Jesus. They would be free to live their lives without guilt, without depression, and without being driven back into sin. What would be wrong with that? A true Christian is exited to talk about Jesus to anyone from any religion, or culture, or nationality, or color ... anytime, anywhere.

18

Chapter Eighteen

THE CURSE OF DEAD RELIGION

Do not be deceived. You are no greater in God's eyes because you are, or are not Amish. God is no respecter of persons and He does not recognize your religion. God only recognizes your heart after you have accepted Jesus in a real way. The righteousness of any religion cannot be justified by its antiquity. If this were so, Islam and Catholicism would be more righteous than most of today's institutionalized religions, including any of the Amish and Mennonite sects. God does not kill off these dead religions. He uses them as His winnowing fan, to purge His threshing floor (See Luke 3:17). Think of it this way, all these dead religions, and the "fun" churches, are like magnets that suck up the chaff from the wheat. This keeps the Church of Christ pure from the chaff that makes it impure.

God does not usually destroy mankind as he did Sodom and Gomorrah (See Genesis. 19). He would even have left those cities stand, if even twenty righteous would have been found in them. So do not think that any religion of today is righteous before God's eyes merely because he lets it stand.

Jesus gave the parable of the harvest field (See Matthew 13:24-30). In that parable these instructions were given.

> *Let both grow together until the harvest: and in the time of harvest*
> *I will say to the reapers, Gather ye together first the tares, and bind*
> *them in bundles to burn them: but gather the wheat into my barn.*
> MATTHEW 13:30, KJV

God lets both the evil and the good church dwell side by side. The sheep and the goats graze in the same pasture.

Imagine how many children could have been saved from an awful death from the great flood if their parents had heeded the warning call of Noah. They perished, not because of their own sins but because of those of their parents and forefathers. The Old Testament law said—

> *Keeping mercy for thousands, forgiving iniquity and transgression*
> *and sin, and that will by no means clear the guilty; visiting the*
> *iniquity of the fathers upon the children, and upon the children's*
> *children, unto the third and to the fourth generation.*
> EXODUS 34:7, KJV

But Jesus became that curse for us, in our place, for all who accept Him in a real, truly born again way

> *Christ hath redeemed us from the curse of the*
> *law, being made a curse for us: for it is written,*
> *Cursed is every one that hangeth on a tree.*
> GALATIANS 3:13, KJV

He not only redeemed us from our sins. He redeemed us from the curse of the law as well (See Galatians 3:13). Those who will not give up their own life and take up the cross to follow Him daily are not freed from the curse of the law. Depriving one's children of the Gospel of Jesus Christ intentionally is comparable to those parents in Noah's time. So too is depriving one's children unintentionally by forcing them to listen to a language they cannot clearly understand. This prevents children from coming to know Jesus.

Noah, like Moses, was an Old Testament shadow—a likeness of Jesus Christ. They each had a salvation message and a means by which people could escape the impending doom. Only Jesus Christ has the salvation message that brings eternal life with the Father. Who would deprive their children of such a wonderful Gospel message? Only those like the people of Noah's time who were too wrapped up in their own pagan worship. Or, they are like the Pharisees in Jesus time, who were so indoctrinated by their own man made version of righteousness, they completely missed the Messiah, even though He walked in their midst.

If they had followed the true teachings of the Old Testament, they would never have missed Him. The Old Testament faithfully pointed forward to Jesus Christ. If the Jews, or the Amish, would actually read the law and the prophets for what they are intended to proclaim, they would all eventually come to Jesus. They would abandon their ordinances of men for a new law written on their hearts. Yet, because of the traditional commandments of men, they were not even following the written law. They have established a perverted mutation of the commandments of God, adding their own versions of righteousness to it. Yet they made no more of a mess out of the Old Testament laws than today's religions have made out of the New Testament. Both Old and New point to Jesus. But today's religions have utterly perverted the Gospel of Jesus. Their distortions of truth are as bad, and probably even worse, than those the Scribes and Pharisees worked into the Old Testament interpretations.

Like them, these New Testament Pharisees did so by adding their own thoughts and ideas of how they wished to teach.

The results are a falling away. Just look at what has happened to the Jews and their children. This has been brought upon themselves by their own curse at the crucifixion of Jesus Christ.

> *Then answered all the people, and said, His*
> *blood be on us, and on our children.*
> MATTHEW 27:25, KJV

The desolation of Jerusalem, prophesied by the prophet Daniel (See Daniel 9), and executed by the Roman Emperor Titus, came to the very ones who condemned Jesus. They brought the curse upon themselves and their innocent children

In A.D. 70, Titus, who was a centurion of the Roman legions and later became emperor of Rome, led a campaign against Jerusalem. This period of history is called the Judean Wars. These wars essentially destroyed all that was Jerusalem less than one full generation after the death of Jesus Christ. In the midst of the campaign, the temple in Jerusalem was burned and destroyed. Its walls were broken down, just as Jesus had prophesied. History relates that over 1,000,000 people were killed by Titus' armies, and more than 90,000 people were taken into slavery. Today, all that remains of the temple is the Western wall, where orthodox Jews go to pray. On top of the temple mount, where the ancient temple stood, is a mosque—The Dome of the Rock—one of Islam's holiest sites.

This curse seems to continually hover over the Jews, even until today. They never repented of the curse they proclaimed against themselves. The Holocaust, a systematic extermination of Jews waged by Hitler's Nazi regime during World War II is just one example.

Millions of Jews were killed, imprisoned, or driven from Russia by the rise of Communism in the early 1900's. Again and again throughout history, the Jews have been singled out for persecution and destruction. But this curse brought on through dead and false religion is even worse than the desolation of Jerusalem.

Think of all the helpless victims who will go to hell for eternity. Think of those who, because their parents denied them the Gospel message of Jesus Christ, will also go to hell. Think of those who will not come to Christ because they are instructed in a language they cannot understand.

The Gospel message is not one of condemnation and should never be brought forth as one. It is not meant to instill the fear of hell and eternal punishment into young minds. It is God's message of hope and love, of forgiveness, and faith in our eternal Savior. If these truths are brought out and taught to our children from their infancy, they will learn to fear God in a healthy, respectful way. They will automatically fear His judgment.

Only through the teaching of a simple Gospel message will we ever be able to break the generational curses passed down by the sins of our forefathers. These curses are seen and felt when a young man falls into sin. People shake their heads as they talk gossip about the one who has fallen. Yet, he is merely repeating the sins as his father and even his grandfathers. They will say something like: "It's just too bad that he had to turn out like his father." But if this young man were born again,

> *Only through the teaching of a simple Gospel message will we ever be able to break generational curses.*

he could break free from that bondage. He could throw off those chains that bind him to the sins of his fathers. And that is the only way it will happen.

All too often boys who fall into sexual immorality in their lives have a father who has the same problem. No matter how subtle that problem may be, it is there. These curses are serious, and the demons that feed on them are real. They tend to become worse and worse unless Jesus is invited into his life and comes in to convert him.

We should not be deceived any more by plain clothes or humble lifestyles. While the fruits of true Christianity include modest, conservative dress, being comfortable in simple, undecorated houses, eating wholesome, simple diets, etc., true Christianity is not about these things. Christianity does not begin with a lifestyle. It begins with a life change. It is the change which produces the fruit, not the other way around.

Not having true discernment about issues such as smoking, allowing it as long as it is controlled by the doctrines of men, is the result of a seriously dead religion. Preachers must quit preaching "dos and don'ts" and begin to preach the salvation message of Jesus Christ. That is what draws people to get their hearts right with the Lord. The results are hearts moved with conviction not to sin anymore. People see for themselves the right from the wrong. Rules do not convict the heart, they only endorse guilt. There are always those moments "out behind the barn," away from the prying eyes of those who enforce the rules.

For the person who truly follows hard after God there is no "out behind the barn." That person realizes in his heart that God will be present anywhere and everywhere. The difference on the inside will direct us the good and the evil that will determine where we stand on the Day of Judgment. There the judge, Jesus Christ, will separate the sheep (those who willingly follow Him) from the goats (those who must be herded). Our lives speak for themselves.

Are you part of a dead religion? You can be honest with yourself. No one is going to hear your response to this question but God and you. No one needs to hear you say it for it to be so. Our fruits speak for themselves.

We will all receive a mark upon our foreheads. Call it whatever you will, mythical, mystical, or physical, but it will happen according to the word of God.

> *And I looked, and, lo, a Lamb stood on the mount Sion,*
> *and with Him an hundred forty and four thousand,*
> *having his Father's name written in their foreheads.*
> REVELATION 14:1, KJV

The Father's name will be written, or—

> *... for those who are deceived. And the third angel followed*
> *them, saying with a loud voice, If any man worship the beast and*
> *his image, and receive his mark in his forehead, or in his hand,*
> *The same shall drink of the wine of the wrath of God, which*
> *is poured out without mixture into the cup of his indignation;*
> *and he shall be tormented with fire and brimstone in the*
> *presence of the holy angels, and in the presence of the Lamb:*
> *And the smoke of their torment ascendeth up forever and ever:*
> *and they have no rest day nor night, who worship the beast and*
> *his image, and whosoever receiveth the mark of his name.*
> REVELATION 14:9-11, KJV

This life is not a joke. It is not about fun and games. It is not about doing things for fun to make us happy. It is not about being everyone's buddy or friend. There is no value in living the best you can, while you hope you can make it into heaven. Life goes far deeper and is far more serious than all of this.

This life is about finding Jesus in a real way. Do not be uncomfortable to speak about the greatness of Jesus. Do not refuse to acknowledge the fact that someone can actually be born again and know the free pardon from their sin. If you are one of those who are afraid to leave the Amish, or some other plain religion, you do not yet have the true salvation of Jesus in your life. The Apostle Paul was raised as a Jew. He was a Pharisee and a scholar who forsook it all to follow Jesus. In Romans chapter 11, he described the difference between dead religion and true Christian life. He compared these two things to the grafting of a branch into an olive tree.

Do not be uncomfortable to speak about the greatness of Jesus.

> *For if thou wert cut out of the olive tree which is wild*
> *by nature, and wert grafted contrary to nature into a*
> *good olive tree: how much more shall these, which be the*
> *natural branches, be grafted into their own olive tree?*
> ROMANS 11:24, KJV)

It is important to read the entire passage in order to get the full meaning of what he is saying here. The Apostle Paul clearly taught against the law being used by born again believers as a path to heaven.

> *But if ye be led of the Spirit, ye are not under the law.*
> GALATIANS 5:18, KJV

We should not be part of an apostate church (See 2 Corinthians 6:14, KJV). We can also read how Paul abandoned his linage to follow Jesus. He even called his old life dung (See Philippians 3:5-8). The first Christians were not raised up as Christians. They became Christians by accepting Jesus Christ as Lord and Savior. They forsook everything to follow Him, including their former religion. That is what made them Christians in the first place.

Why then would it be sin to leave a church or religion for the sake of the Gospel? The Jews, the Pharisees, and the Romans killed Jesus and all of the apostles for the same reasons. The same demonic spirit of the antichrist dwells in the hearts of the men that have controlled the Roman Catholic, Islamic, Amish, Mormon, Hutterite and many other religions ever since Jesus' time on earth. That same spirit of antichrist will remain with us until the end.

Satan is the one who was cast out from heaven because of his exalted attitude of hierarchy. He is the one for whom hell was created. He is the one that instigated the curse in the garden of Eden. And he is the very one responsible for the death of every single holy martyr ever killed since the beginning of time, beginning with righteous Able, and whose final name has yet to be recorded. Satan is the one who has deceived multiplied millions and caused many religions to compromise with the truth. They have made their own rules and have caused many to fear them rather than God. And Satan blinds them to it.

Satan is the one who, along with his angels and those he deceived by his cunningly devised fables, will burn forever and ever in the torment of hell.

And the smoke of their torment ascendeth up forever and ever: and they have no rest day nor night, who worship the beast and his image, and whosoever receiveth the mark of his name.
REVELATION 14:11, KJV

Chapter Nineteen

DENOMINATIONAL BARRIERS

There are many different churches today with many different names that distinguish them from one another. There are thousands of churches in the world that profess to be serving the same God. We have the Methodists, the Baptists, the Presbyterians, and the Pentecostals. There are Churches of Christ, Churches of God, Episcopal, and Luthren. The list goes on and on. Among plain folk, one finds Amish, a variety of Mennonites, River Brethren, Fellowship, Charity, and Hutterites, just to name a few.

There actually is nothing of itself wrong with being identified by our different names. There is certainly nothing wrong with going to different churches. There would be something very wrong with our Christianity if we all fit in the same building, lived in the same community, or even understood everything exactly the same. To do that would be to isolate ourselves from the rest of the world. Then there would be no one to take the Gospel message of Jesus Christ and preach it to all the world. But that is what Jesus commanded us to.

Actually, we need to be spread out. We need to keep our churches from getting too full by sending people out to start outreach churches and mission centers. The first church that we read about in the book of Acts had all things in common. They sold their possessions, gave it to a common treasury, ate together, and apparently were all together as one big family (see Acts 2:42-47). While this was a good way to get the church off to a running start, it was not to last forever. This common gathering was beneficial to disciple all those young converts and train them to be seasoned, tried ministers. It was never God's plan that we should all be together in one place or have only one church assembly on this earth and in this time. That is for our eternal home in heaven.

For this time on earth we are called to be soldiers of the cross. We are to carry the Gospel message to every corner of the world and proclaim it to every creature.

> *And he said unto them, Go ye into all the world,*
> *and preach the gospel to every creature.*
> MARK 16:15, KJV

For the sake of the Gospel, the church was sent out into different parts of the world. This is how the Apostle Paul was sent to preach the message of Christ to the Gentiles. His letters, which make up much of the New Testament, were written to the churches he had established. These churches were identified by their different city names, not by some denominational title. The Corinthian church was in the city of Corinth. The Roman church was in Rome. And the Ephesian church was in Ephesus.

This diversity of churches was neither designed nor intended to cause the denominational barriers we know today. Paul encouraged believers to remain united in their hearts and to love one another.

For by one Spirit are we all baptized into one body,
whether we be Jews or Gentiles, whether we be bond or
free; and have been all made to drink into one Spirit.
1 CORINTHIANS 12:13, KJV

We who are born again will be united. We will be in one accord and in one Spirit because we have become a part of the Kingdom of God. We enter through the washing by the Blood of the Lamb of God, Jesus Christ.

For as many of you as have been baptized into Christ have put on
Christ. There is neither Jew nor Greek, there is neither bond nor free,
there is neither male nor female: for ye are all one in Christ Jesus.
GALATIANS 3:27-28, KJV

So, how can we relate this "all one in Christ Jesus" to the many denominations we know today? The Bible does not teach different, or multiple doctrines. Yet, denominations have erected barriers between themselves and their fellow Christians because of doctrinal difference.

The Bible does determine that we should separate ourselves from unbelievers, false prophets, and teachers of strange doctrines. But look at who has taken the lead raising up denominational barriers. It is the plain religions. They have obviously moved far from the truth. Their barriers are not for protection from the world as much as for keeping their membership under their control. They try to convince themselves and others as well, that theirs is the only truly righteous religion. Yet because of their departure from biblical truth to man-made rules, they have become controlling cults.

These barriers are all over trivial things—the wearing of beards and the possession and driving of cars. These are all material things and of no consequence when compared to a man's soul. But there is only one Gospel for us all, and it is not a gospel of dos and don'ts.

> *Wherefore if ye be dead with Christ from the rudiments of the world,*
> *why, as though living in the world, are ye subject to ordinances,*
> *(Touch not; taste not; handle not; Which all are to perish with*
> *the using;) after the commandments and doctrines of men?*
> COLOSSIANS 2:20-22, KJV

Amish and Mennonites will not fellowship with each other because of their doctrinal differences. Something as trivial as whether or not you wear a beard can determine if you can worship together. On and on it goes. It's all about doctrine ... rules, *ordnung*, "brotherly agreements." Whatever they can argue and disagree about, they do. Even different Amish sects contradict one another's doctrines and refuse to fellowship with each other because of it. Old Order Mennonites are no different; they all do the same thing.—cars or buggies, black cars only, black cars with all the chrome painted black, black buggies, gray buggies, and the list goes on forever. They are not arguing about God, for they know far too little about Him. Their arguments are all about commandments of men, things that have nothing to do with salvation at all.

Jesus spoke against being bound by the commandments of men, so they are all wrong in doing this. They might as well all go to the same church and be labeled as false prophets. That would be better than giving all of Christianity a bad reputation.

All of these religions have lost everything that their forefathers worked so hard to achieve. Not just the Amish and Mennonites who won't fellowship with one another because of their contradictions. The hard won victories of the Reformation times in the 1600s are overlooked as well. The forefathers they so proudly profess to follow would be ashamed.

If they could see how their descendants are acting, they would be utterly disbelieving. These descendants now have little more than a cursed mess to deal with. Things have gone so far out of hand the churches look nothing like they did when they were first formed. Rules and regulations have replaced relationship and what remains is but a faint shadow of what was.

Notice the enmity and strife which exists between various Amish denominations. The Lancaster (PA) Conference of Amish will not fellowship with a particular Ohio sect of Amish, even though their doctrine is very close. No one really remembers why the enmity arose. It developed many years ago between forefathers, but today there is very little if any fellowship. However, the Lancaster Amish will gladly fellowship with another group, in this case a New York sect which only recently suffered a sexual molestation case.

The Bishop tried his best to cover it all up, going so far as to order everyone to tell the N.Y. State Police it was just a rumor. That didn't work. The case was already well under investigation before the people were able to lie to the police. The case was officially resolved, and the Amish community gladly swept the whole affair "under the rug" The father of the six year old girl who was molested was quickly excommunicated and is no longer Amish. Through it all, however, there have been multiple cases where women, and even men and boys have reported the same thing. Some who are older also confessed that they too had been sexually molested. In some cases, the molestation was by a deceased grandfather or uncle who never took the opportunity to repent.

There are many examples of the denominational barriers erected by the clergy of these communist ruled religions. It is difficult to appreciate a culture that is very strict about shunning, yet who cover such acts. Many of those who have seen the utterly perverted and dark evil that goes on behind closed doors have left them for a Christian church, and for the sake of the Gospel. Now, they too are shunned.

The fact that there is sin in these churches is not the problem. Many churches are faced with humiliating sins from time to time. But it is the way that these sins are dealt with which demonstrates how far these religions have fallen from God. All churches have problems. That is because churches are made up of people, and people are not perfect. Leaders need to seek God through much fasting and prayer to help them resolve their problems. That is how the difference can be shown. Those who hear and know Gods voice, and follow it will always see real results. Those who rely on the *ordnung* as their systematic method to deal with sin, fall short again and again.

> *As soon as anyone sees the truth and begins to question the system or the leaders, that individual is quickly excommunicated.*

Theirs is a system which operates the same way with or without God in it. It is a system in which it does not matter who agrees or disagrees, nothing will change, As soon as anyone sees the truth and begins to question the system or the leaders, that individual is quickly excommunicated. Therefore their Godly men are quickly cast out. Little wonder that things are handled in the way they are, or covered up to prevent embarrassment or exposure.

Whatever became of following Jesus? Or with seeking Him? What has become of hearing a brother's questions and responding honestly without fear or intimidation? Why should people not be able to question how things are handled when they do not line up with the true Word of God? Maybe that brother's understanding would help the church move closer to God, not further away. But these things never seem to happen this way in an orthodox religion.

Their churches have been built with wood, hay and stubble. Over the years they have become propped up with flimsy props and patched with cheap patches. They have built tall fences to hold the membership because they have no other way to keep them. They will consider no one else's advice, especially those who would so willingly point them to Jesus for answers. Instead they just keep adding more props, patches, more fences to hold what the others failed to hold their already weakened religion together.

These systems are what caused these denominational barriers to spring up in the first place. It was these disagreements between brothers and churches, disagreements over the trivial doctrines of men. It was these disagreements between brothers and churches who at one time held communion together. They visited and preached in one another's churches, enjoyed one another's company, and shared a common faith. Now they just disagree.

True, we need to use Godly discernment about who we fellowship with and with whom we hold communion. We certainly need discernment about who allow to preach from our pulpits. We must be aware of false prophets. But none of this discernment has a single thing to do with facial hair, or rubber tires, or how people dress. The saying that a plain dress is the result of a humble heart is deceptive indeed.

Who is more proud? The man with a flashy shirt, or the plain dressed man who hides his proud heart and stubborn will behind plain clothes? Modest is good. Modesty is biblical, But modesty begins in the heart, not on the clothesline. It is true that Christians will wear modest clothing but they are not the only ones that do. A haughty attitude covered with plain clothes is still a wolf in sheep's clothing.

> *Beware of false prophets, which come to you in sheep's*
> *clothing, but inwardly they are ravening wolves.*
> MATTHEW 7:15, KJV

This is why Jesus said,

> *Judge not according to the appearance, but judge righteous judgment.*
> JOHN 7:24, KJV

These plainly clothed people may believe they please God with their dress, but God is not interested in dress. He is interested in our souls. The Amish preach that they must wear plain clothing to be a light to the world. But the world does not care. What a disgusting way to evangelize.

Still, it comes as no surprise that they should believe and teach this. The Pharisees also believed and taught after the same manner, much to the dismay of Jesus who warned against this.

> *But all their works they do for to be seen of men: they make broad*
> *their phylacteries, and enlarge the borders of their garments,*
> MATTHEW 23:5, KJV

While dressing in costly, immodest, formfitting, flashy clothes and jewelry may not portray a humble heart, neither do clothes that are intentionally made extra plain demonstrate any level of humility. Jesus opened the way for all. He is no respecter of persons. Neither will he judge according to the clothing someone is wearing to prove their righteousness.

For by one Spirit are we all baptized into one body,
whether we be Jews or Gentiles, whether we be bond or
free; and have been all made to drink into one Spirit.
1 CORINTHIANS 12:13, KJV

This verse says that it does not matter who or what you are, if you truly follow Jesus you are a part of the Kingdom. Therefore if you are bound to, or if you are one of the dictators who enforces the rules that make you a certain denomination, you will have no part in the Kingdom of heaven. You have segregated yourself from the only one true church. In the Kingdom of God there is no differentiation between Jews and Gentiles, between Amish or English. There is only freedom in Christ where no one is bound by man-made rules and *ordnung*.

There is neither Jew nor Greek, there is neither bond nor free,
there is neither male nor female: for ye are all one in Christ Jesus.
GALATIANS 3:28, KJV

What then do you suppose will happen to these institutionalized religions in a Kingdom where "... all are one in Christ Jesus?" (Galatians 3:28). This even pertains to those bishops and elders who observe and preserve those denominational barriers which Jesus removed by his death on the cross. It is these blind guides, the bishops and elders, who have re-established the extra-Biblical doctrines of man.

Some of these churches continue to fellowship with sexually immoral people. They tolerate those who refrain from teaching children all there is to know about the Bible., while forcing separation between husband and wife because the husband became born again—in some cases by physical force (this is a sad, true story). Surely, they should be able to have fellowship with a church whose men are clean shaven. Or better yet, why not use some Godly discernment about who they actually do fellowship with?

No one wants to fellowship with obviously corrupted churches. Nor should we, but the question needs to be answered. Who is on what list? One thing is certain. Any religion that judges from outward appearances without looking to the heart is already on the corrupt list.

People only have a limited, allotted time table to get their priorities straight and to repent before God before He gives them over to a reprobate mind

> *For the wrath of God is revealed from heaven against all ungodliness and unrighteousness of men, who hold the truth in unrighteousness; Because that which may be known of God is manifest in them; for God hath shewed it unto them. For the invisible things of him from the creation of the world are clearly seen, being understood by the things that are made, even his eternal power and Godhead; so that they are without excuse: Because that, when they knew God, they glorified him not as God, neither were thankful; but became vain in their imaginations, and their foolish heart was darkened. Professing themselves to be wise, they became fools, And changed the glory of the uncorruptible God into an image made like to corruptible man, and to birds, and fourfooted beasts, and creeping things. Wherefore God also gave them up to uncleanness through the lusts of their own hearts, to dishonour their own bodies between themselves: Who changed the truth of God into a lie, and worshipped and served the creature more than the Creator, who is blessed forever. Amen. For this cause God gave them up unto vile affections: for even their women did change the natural use into that which is against nature: And likewise also the men, leaving the natural use of the*

woman, burned in their lust one toward another; men with men working that which is unseemly, and receiving in themselves that recompence of their error which was meet. And even as they did not like to retain God in their knowledge, God gave them over to a reprobate mind, to do those things which are not convenient;
ROMANS 1:18-28, KJV

Some of these religions have already missed it. Others are very near to it, and time is running out. These churches and their leaders should come back to reality and cut down the extra- Biblical religious barriers that Jesus cut down. It was unrighteous to erect them in the first place.

It is time to restore the church to the way Jesus intended it to be

For he is our peace, who hath made both one, and hath broken down the middle wall of partition between us; Having abolished in his flesh the enmity, even the law of commandments contained in ordinances; for to make in himself of twain one new man, so making peace; And that he might reconcile both unto God in one body by the cross, having slain the enmity thereby: And came and preached peace to you which were afar off, and to them that were nigh.

For through him we both have access by one Spirit unto the Father. Now therefore ye are no more strangers and foreigners, but fellow citizens with the saints, and of the household of God; And are built upon the foundation of the apostles and prophets, Jesus Christ himself being the chief corner stone.
EPHESIANS 2:14-20, KJV

Notice how he writes in verse 20" Jesus Christ Himself being the chief cornerstone?" It is Jesus, not bishops who is the foundation and Chief stone of corner in the church. Therefore we must follow Him and not a bishop who teaches anything different than what Jesus Himself taught. Be determined to only submit yourself to the one who watches over your soul in a Christ-like manner. Follow Christ only, and walk with those who walk with Christ.

Chapter Twenty

FREEDOM OF RELIGION

America was founded on the basis of religious freedom. This principle is part of our Constitution, written and enacted by the founders of this country. Nearly all of the founders had their origins in the European countries from which they had fled. They were taking refuge in a land where they were free to worship their Lord Jesus Christ. Their vision was to be able to serve and worship the Lord without being under the control of a domineering governmental authority—not only free from kings and queens, but also from state controlled churches, especially the Roman Catholic Church. Many have suffered rejection and persecution at the hands of the Church. So they came, enduring the hardship and danger of sea travel during the 1600s. They risked illness, starvation, stormy seas, and the opposition of native peoples, just for the freedom to worship God, unhindered by the world around them.

Churches were founded and thrived in a land where there was less religious persecution to hinder their growth. Then in the year of 1728, the Amish came to America. Their founder was Jacob Ammann, who had led them in a split from the Swiss Brethren in the 1690s. This was because of disagreements in church discipline. Jacob Ammann was an extremely temperamental and feisty reformer who refused to bow to anyone or their ideas. His mode of convincing others to follow him was not unlike that of the Islamic founder Mohammad. There was a difference in their modes of enlisting and maintaining followers, however. Mohammed killed or maimed those who refused to follow him. Jacob Ammann's method was to give them over to the devil.

The sobering thought is this. Both of these false prophets still have followers. In the case of Mohammed, more than a billion souls are under Islamic beliefs. The Amish have far less numbers because they do not recruit or enlist people to adopt their way of life. They simply impose their way on their children through man-made rules, intimidation, and fear.

Both religions are still persecuting Christians. Muslims are torturing and killing them. The Amish are giving them over to the devil for the destruction of the flesh. This idea of handing unrepentant sinners over to Satan for the destruction of the flesh originated with the Apostle Paul. He did it out of heartfelt, loving concern for a wayward, unrepentant sinner who was in an incestuous situation (See 1 Corinthians. 5:5). His concern was that the soul of that individual would be saved in the day of our Lord. Ammann took it to another level. He seemed to think he too had the power to go around handing people over to Satan, for whatever reason he chose. And he did—a lot.

At one time he excommunicated some five hundred of his Mennonite brethren for not conforming to his doctrine. These poor excommunicated Mennonites were terrified and lived in a state of desperate mental anguish. At that time, even the thought of being excommunicated, no matter what the reason or who performed the act, was next to being cast into hell itself. Moreover, Ammann refused to lift the *bann* off of them. Eventually they realized that Ammann's excommunications were unjustified and harmless. They realized he was just a temperamental man, throwing childish tantrums to get his own way.

To be excommunicated for an unrepentant sin is be forced to live in a fearful way. It should not be ignored or taken lightly. But to be excommunicated because of some dictatorial agenda is actually a fulfillment of the prediction Jesus made. He forewarned His disciples of the persecutions they, and by extension, all of Christianity would suffer.

They shall put you out of the synagogues: yea, the time cometh,
that whosoever killeth you will think that he doeth God service.
JOHN 16:2, KJV

People who do not understand the difference between these two extremes can easily be controlled by dictatorial leaders. They use this form of excommunication to instill the fear of hell into people. Thus they can control them to conform to their will. Most of these dictators do not even realize how far they are removed from God. But that is because they refuse to submit themselves fully to Christ and be born again.

Ammann was no exception. In all probability, he believed he was doing this for God. Yet if Ammann, or his followers would have actually known Jesus, they would have had a completely different attitude.

And these things will they do unto you, because
they have not known the Father, nor me.
JOHN 16:3, KJV

Excommunicating people is serious business. It should never be taken lightly. Neither should it be a means to control people's lives. Rather, it should cause people to see the error of their ways. Furthermore, such errors should clearly be biblically defined, unrepentant sin. Not for violating the commandments of men. This is a kind of social death dealing that these religions use to control people. The outright killing of Christians would never get past the government, but excommunication is rather common in America. Most, if not all known cults have this practice, including the (Fundamentalist Latter Day Saints) which is extremist Mormonism, the Amish, many other plain religions, and even many Mennonites.

This evil method of control is a masterpiece of Satan's design. It happens not only in America, it also happens in countries where the governing leadership cannot simply get away with killing people outright. Still, it places people under bondage in order to prevent them from seeing the light of Jesus Christ. In countries controlled by Islam, the law justifies the killing of Christians, so excommunication over doctrinal difference is not much of a consideration. There they treasure each other far too greatly to spend time bickering about hats and beards. In those countries, Christians are genuine and filled with God. No one would risk being a true Christian unless they are sold out to Christ, willing to suffer and die for their faith.

Once churches were established in a free land, Satan readily deceived those that otherwise would have prospered in the Gospel. His tactics included the very freedom they so desired, Being freed from the persecution they had suffered, they soon lost their focus on the Lord, made prosperity their focus and turned toward the lusts of the world. Without persecution to weed out lukewarm Christians, and with plenty of money to validate God's blessing, the churches quickly lost their focus on Christ and fell asleep. Rules were made to keep members in place because waning hearts no longer sought or relied on the Holy Spirit to convict them of righteousness.

Leaders became dictatorial in their efforts to keep the church from going away from Christ. They saw what was happening, but instead of turning their hearts fully to the Lord, they compromised and made rules to keep people in line. They tried to do what the Holy Spirit was sent to do, but couldn't. They could never bring true conviction to people's hearts. So, fear of retribution took the place of holy conviction. Men came to fear other men more than they feared God. Choices regarding personal righteousness were based on consequences that would be suffered by the hand of man. The judgment of God would only be at death, but the judgment of man was immediate and severe.

This became the controlling spirit of the American plain religions. Serving man rather than God is a very strong method of control. It caused those religions to fall back into the same dark deception that had blinded the Pharisees and Roman Catholics before them. The Pharisees and Catholics persecuted their people and justified doing so by their own doctrine instead of the Word of God. The Amish, along with many other religions, do exactly the same thing. Yet, all along they think they are different and would never do the things the Pharisees and the Catholics did.

> *Woe unto you, scribes and Pharisees, hypocrites! because ye*
> *build the tombs of the prophets, and garnish the sepulchers of*
> *the righteous, And say, If we had been in the days of our fathers,*
> *we would not have been partakers with them in the blood of*
> *the prophets. Wherefore ye be witnesses unto yourselves, that*
> *ye are the children of them which killed the prophets. Fill ye*
> *up then the measure of your fathers. Ye serpents, ye generation*
> *of vipers, how can ye escape the damnation of hell?*
> MATTHEW 23:29-33, KJV

Notice that Jesus was addressing the Pharisees. It was not they personally who killed the prophets, or who even killed Jesus. The Jewish system, leaders and priests had destroyed prophets from ancient times. And the Jewish leaders incited the Romans, the ones they considered worldly and not holy, to execute Jesus. But they were responsible. Not specifically holding a stone, or driving a nail, or casting a spear did not free them from guilt."Crucify him," the death sentence of condemnation came from their lips.

This bears a striking resemblance to how Amish skirt their own rules. They hire people in the world (the English) to drive cars for them because they consider driving a car to be a sin. But riding in a car with an unbelieving person is not. They have cellular telephones, computers, internet access, and many other modern conveniences, things they consider to be sinful. But to prevent those being sin, they have them purchased and kept in some worldly person's name.

How they exalt themselves! They think the people of the world are so far beneath them spiritually that they can pay sinners to sin for them. Can sinners go to hell for them, too? Or do they think there are two different Gods or two different plans for salvation?

There is no other way to describe it. They believe the "English" people are already going to hell. If they also go to hell for providing the Amish with conveniences of sin without the consequences of sin, that's not an Amish problem. Don't sin ... get someone to sin for you and you'll be okay. How foolish.

These are the people who proclaim humble submission to the government. They preach such submission in their churches. Yet they are unconstitutionally denying people the very freedom of religion their forefathers came to America to seek. They excommunicate, (socially execute) anyone who wishes to leave the church for the sake of the Gospel. Their resentment spills out against anyone who questions their self-ordained status as gods over people.

Actually this is rebellion against God. More specifically, it is rebellion against God's Word to impose their rules above the clear teachings of Scripture.

> *Blessed are ye, when men shall hate you, and when they shall*
> *separate you from their company, and shall reproach you, and*
> *cast out your name as evil, for the Son of man's sake. Rejoice ye*
> *in that day, and leap for joy: for, behold, your reward is great in*
> *heaven: for in the like manner did their fathers unto the prophets.*
> LUKE 6:22-2, 3 KJV

Rebellion is a serious sin, comparable to witchcraft. Coupled with the stubbornness not to change or to accept God's Word, it is serious indeed

> *. For rebellion is as the sin of witchcraft, and stubbornness is*
> *as iniquity and idolatry. Because thou hast rejected the word*
> *of the LORD, he hath also rejected thee from being king.*
> 1 SAMUEL 15:23, KJV

It goes almost without saying that the world will persecute the church. That is a simple fact. But the Church of Christ has no reason or call to persecute anyone, much less its own. These plain religions, along with Mohammad and Ammann, are worldly systems. If they weren't they would not excommunicate Christians. They believe they are separate from the

The Church of Christ has no reason or call to persecute anyone, much less its own.

world, yet, they are just like the world from which they profess to keep themselves so pure.

The Amish do everything in their power to befriend the world so that they do not lose their drivers and their surrogate conveniences. They preach in their sermons that it is important to be plain because the world expects it. We are called to be a light to the world, not a friend. There is a difference. But clothing is not a form of light. So who are they serving? They are like the blind leading the blind. The preachers preach fables and the sleepy membership submits in mute, blind submission. Yet they are all wrapped up in the world with their businesses, politics, voting, protesting governments, etc. They are very similar to the church which, with open arms, invited Constantine and his throng of pagan friends into their midst to avoid worldly inflicted pain. They are no different than the Pharisees, the Roman Catholics, the other various persecutors throughout the bloody theater of the dark ages, and Mohammad with his bloody followers.

Today, persecution comes in a more subtle way. It comes by condemning someone to eternal damnation in hell. It comes by causing him to believe he is hopelessly lost. Unless and until he breaks down and comes back to the prelates, weeping and begging for mercy, he has no hope whatsoever. Requiring people to confess to the clergy is no less than Satan convincing people that a man, not Jesus, provides salvation. Either that, or that salvation from Jesus only comes through the prelates.

> *Neither is there salvation in any other: for there is none other name*
> *under heaven given among men, whereby we must be saved.*
> ACTS 4:12, KJV

This is nothing more than a form of communism within the church. It must be avoided. However, this is not to be confused with biblically defined confession. It is necessary to confess our sins to those whom we have offended. It is also necessary to humble ourselves and repent of our faults to one another. We need to do this in the fear of God, but we do not need to come before a panel of bishops in order for God to forgive our sins.

In 1428 a group of reformed Christian men were taken into custody by order of their king. They were accused of heresies. One of them was the well known preacher William White, who wrote a confession of faith. It included these statements as a part of that testimony.

- (4) Than auricular confession is not necessary and that one need not go and confess to the priests but to God alone; since no one has the power to forgive a sinner his sins.

- (7) That no one is bound on pain of damnation to observe lent or any other fast days commanded by the Roman Church.

- (11) That the excommunications and ecclesiastical punishments decreed by the prelates are not to be regarded.

- (21) It is no sin to oppose the commands of the (Roman) church.

- (22) That the (true) Catholic (catholic means universal or world wide) church is only the congregation of the beloved children of God.

(*Martyrs Mirror* page 346, parentheses added)

These articles demonstrate how William White and his brethren refused to conform to the Roman Catholic Church which hated them for leaving and proving it wrong. This is how history seems to repeat itself, since those who leave the Amish Church are faced with the exact same things William White and his friends faced.

Another confession of theirs was: (8)That the Pope is the antichrist and that his followers and his prelates disciples of the antichrist and that the pope has no authority to loose or bind on earth.

You can understand why the Christians who wrote this were tortured and killed. You don't need to wonder why so few are being persecuted here in America. Very few are "Christian" enough to stand up to these evil dictators and proclaim the truth, no matter what the consequences are.

These words from history offer a very fitting assessment of today's orthodox religious clergymen who, like dictators, have set themselves up as god-like dictators over the people they are leading. More often than not they impose some self-ordained law upon the members of the church. Such laws have absolutely nothing to do with salvation or righteousness. Yet, they are set forth as such, with the assertion that to disobey any of them is to receive certain damnation, as if God himself had ordained those rules. They often even go as far as to preach that God, in fact, did ordain their rules. This is a lie, conceived by that liar the devil, and impressed into the minds of men. These lies keep people from the truth as the prelates equate their rules with the true word of God. You must be willing to see the deception behind all of it if you want the truth to guide your heart.

This type of religious hierarchy has been going on for hundreds, even thousands of years. They thrive and become ever larger. They even look righteous to carnal man. But do not be deceived. This is not at all what Jesus said His church would look like.

How is it that so many of today's religions completely miss this? Do they believe we do not live in this era anymore? Or, perhaps that God changed the way things are done? Perhaps they believe another Savior came and established another covenant.

The truth is that they have fallen asleep, fallen away from God, and rejected the prompting of the Holy Spirit. They have denied the deity of Jesus Christ and have gone on to establish their own version of righteousness. Their form of righteousness will one day force them to hear the voice of Jesus.

> *Many will say to me in that day, Lord, Lord, have we not prophesied in thy name? and in thy name have cast out devils? and in thy name done many wonderful works? And then will I profess unto them, I never knew you: depart from me, ye that work iniquity.*
> MATTHEW 7:22-23, KJV

Sadly very few of these people will ever see the truth. They will miss it for the same reason that the Pharisees never saw Jesus for who he was. They cannot see righteousness unless it comes in a form that resembles what they have established as righteousness. Outside of this box, they will never see the truth. They have blinded themselves in their own deceit.

> *In whom the god of this world hath blinded the minds of them which believe not, lest the light of the glorious gospel of Christ, who is the image of God, should shine unto them.*
> 2 CORINTHIANS 4:4, KJV

The Bible boldly proclaims the truth, the very Bible they profess to believe. Yet they only see it in a form they want to believe, a form that imitates their version of righteousness. The remainder they simply ignore because they do not understand, or else they simply do not want to understand.

> *Desiring to be teachers of the law; understanding*
> *neither what they say, nor whereof they affirm.*
> 1 Timothy 1:7, KJV

It is time to rise up and expose these liars for who they really are. True Christians should join in. It will not be easy, nor will it be fun. Neither will it likely be very rewarding in this life. Yet if we love as Jesus commanded us to love, we will do it for their sakes, and for the sakes of those ensnared in their webs of deception and dead religion.

The Apostles rejoiced to be counted worthy to suffer for the sake of the Gospel (See Acts 5). So should we, if we are the true sons of God. These false prophets of today are no different than those of Jesus time, no different than those in the times of the early Anabaptists. They have so many things in common. They set themselves up as gods over others. They refuse correction. They cannot see any truth because it does not fit their version of righteousness. They persecute by excommunication, torture, or death those whose lives and words prove them wrong.

These include but are not limited to the Pharisees, the old Roman Catholic Church, the Hutterites, the Mormons, the Muslims, and the Amish. And none of these is more righteousness than the other. They all fall into the same category. Their mode of operation follows what Jesus proclaimed would take place.

> *They shall put you out of the synagogues: yea, the time cometh,*
> *that whosoever killeth you will think that he doeth God service.*
> John 16:2, KJV

Some of the membership of these religions may well be saved if they are given a chance. Many are hopelessly ensnared and long for a way out, yet they remain because of their fear. Jesus foresaw that his true followers would be persecuted for exposing the dark evil of those sheepskin clad wolves. They demand complete submission from their church membership and excommunicate, threaten, maim, kill, and hate us if we choose to follow Jesus Christ. They and their father, the devil, working through them are trying to snuff out all who follow the true form of Christianity. They come as preachers of light, led by one who disguises himself as an angel of light.

> *For such are false apostles, deceitful workers, transforming*
> *themselves into the apostles of Christ. And no marvel; for Satan*
> *himself is transformed into an angel of light. Therefore it is no*
> *great thing if his ministers also be transformed as the ministers*
> *of righteousness; whose end shall be according to their works.*
> 2 CORINTHIANS 11:13-15, KJV

In no way should their haughtiness discourage us from boldly proclaiming the truth and exposing their dark evil, even if it costs us our lives.

> *And fear not them which kill the body, but are not*
> *able to kill the soul: but rather fear him which is*
> *able to destroy both soul and body in hell.*
> MATTHEW 10:28, KJV

We can see, by being exposed to their evil tactics, that we are those of whom Jesus spoke of that would suffer. To stay in a church or religion like that is impossible if we truly follow Christ. The Bible teaches us not to follow the traditions of men.

> *Beware lest any man spoil you through philosophy and vain*
> *deceit, after the tradition of men, after the rudiments of*

the world, and not after Christ. {rudiments: or, elements}
{make a prey: or, seduce you, or, lead you astray}
COLOSSIANS 2:8, KJV

Their doctrine is vain and unscriptural. Many Christians have tried to get them to see the truth, but they refuse to believe. Rather, they put their faith in the traditions of their forefathers like the Pharisees and the Roman Catholics did.

A Christian cannot stay in a church or religion like the Amish and remain true to Christ. On a semi-annual basis the Amish hold communion. Before they are allowed to partake, they are required to restate their allegiance to the *ordnung* and the corrupted church standards. By doing this, they are being "partakers in another man's sins" (1 Timothy 5:22). Sooner or later they will be faced with excommunicating another member, either for being born again and embracing true Christianity, or for confessing a sin that breaches the rules of the *ordnung*—both of which are serious sins (See John 16:2-3 and read John 8.)

John 8 is one example Jesus left for us regarding how we should deal with a repentant sinner. A woman had been caught in adultery—in the very act, Scripture says. The law directed that such a person to be stoned to death ... no question, no trial. But Jesus had a different response.

"He that is without sin among you, let him first cast a stone at her."
JOHN 8:7, KJV

Since Scribes and Pharisees could not condemn her Jesus spoke again.

And Jesus said unto her, "Neither do I condemn thee: go, and sin no more"
JOHN 8:11, KJV

These Scribes and Pharisees, whom Jesus despised, were righteous enough to see the truth. Yet the Amish continue to blindly give repentant sinners over to Satan for the destruction of the flesh. Do they think Jesus himself does not have the power to forgive a sinner? Or that His suffering was not sufficient to forgive a sinner his sins?

You will not find a verse in the New Testament that proves we must give a repentant sinner over to Satan and shun him for six weeks so he can be forgiven. You won't find that he must even be punished in any way. Jesus completely changed the way sin is dealt with. John, Chapter 8, proves this without a doubt. Jesus overruled the Mosiac law when he said "neither do I condemn thee, go and sin no more."

Who are these Amish trying to be when they excommunicate a repentant sinner? Regardless of whether you are the Bishop, the Preacher, the Deacon, or just a member of the church, you have become even more wicked than those Scribes and Pharisees that Jesus confronted. Just from this passage alone, it should be obvious that you cannot possibly remain Amish and be a Christian. A Christian is a follower of Christ and will act towards his fellow man as Christ did.

Unless you are a follower of Jesus Christ, you will go to hell. It is that simple. The wise choice then is to leave the Amish or any other dead religion and accept the salvation of Jesus Christ. You cannot remain in that system because it will destroy you spiritually.

Let no man deceive you with vain words: for because of these things cometh the wrath of God upon the children of disobedience. Be not ye therefore partakers with them. For ye were sometimes darkness, but now are ye light in the Lord: walk as children of light: (For the fruit of the Spirit is in all goodness and righteousness and truth;)

Proving what is acceptable unto the Lord. And have no fellowship
with the unfruitful works of darkness, but rather reprove them.
EPHESIANS 5:6-11, KJV

Nothing in the New Testament justifies the false claim that leaving a particular church or religion is a sin, regardless of any vow one has taken for them. Only religions like Islam, Mormon, Amish, Roman Catholicism, some Mennonites, and all other religious cults will teach and practice such dark deception. No true Christian Church will excommunicate its members should they decide to join another Christian church. There is no reason this practice should be. Yet, because of jealousy, these religions do.

Causing divisions, (1 Corinthians 3:3) controversy, (Isaiah 34:8) and strife (James 3:16) are all sins. But so is envy (jealousy) (James 3:16). Leaving an apostate church for the sake of the Gospel is not a cause of sinful division, controversy, or strife. If it causes jealousy on the part of those left behind, it is not the fault of the Christian who leaves.

There is a way which seemeth right unto a man,
but the end thereof are the ways of death.
PROVERBS 14:12, KJV

Chapter Twenty One

THE LEADER

Jesus did not come to us as a ruler, or to establish an earthly kingdom, although that is what the Jews expected the Messiah to do. He came to serve and to set up His heavenly Kingdom which is His Church. It is made up of those who will follow Him at all costs no matter what the consequences may be. They will be mocked, scorned, excommunicated, beaten, burned, beheaded, hanged, and buried alive. But it is all voluntary. It is a choice.

How fitting that His great Kingdom should be governed in this manner? Even its founder came willingly from heaven, not to be served, but to serve. Jesus is the Head of His bride. Yet He did not come to beat her into submission or to force himself on her. He came to serve her. What a perfect husband! It is our own choice whether to follow Him or not. We must choose which master we will serve. Sadly, if we will not willingly choose, we unwittingly choose. Automatically, because we were all born in sin, we will be serving Satan. But if we choose to follow Christ, we will become Christ-like, and our works will be as the works of Jesus Christ. His offered this commandment.

A new commandment I give unto you, that ye love one
another; as I have loved you, that ye also love one another.
JOHN 13:34, KJV

If we love as Jesus did, we will become servants. We will minister to the sick, feed the hungry, and spread the Gospel message of salvation. Our good works will be centered on what we can do for others. Our works will not have anything to do with trying to please God with our clothes, or what we drive, or how our hair is cut, or whether or not we wear a beard. Only two sacraments were left to the Church by Jesus, communion and baptism in water.

The apostles recognized the ineffectiveness of observing the law for those who have accepted Jesus and are filled with the Holy Ghost.

Forasmuch as we have heard, that certain which went
out from us have troubled you with words, subverting
your souls, saying, Ye must be circumcised, and keep the
law: to whom we gave no such commandment:
ACTS 15:24, KJV

For it seemed good to the Holy Ghost, and to us, to lay upon
you no greater burden than these necessary things; That ye
abstain from meats offered to idols, and from blood, and
from things strangled, and from fornication: from which
if ye keep yourselves, ye shall do well. Fare ye well.
ACTS 15:28-29, KJV

But those verses are completely overlooked by so many church leaders, bishops, preachers, deacons, and elders. They keep right on making up rules however they wish, as though the Bible were not true. It's as if, to them, it doesn't exist. If they read it, they don't understand it, and if they understand it, they don't believe it. Though the scriptures are spiritually discerned (See 1 Corinthians 2:14), no one should have any difficulty understanding that all those rules are spoken against in the Bible. For a bishop, then, to exalt himself over the church is not Christ-like.

> *But Jesus called them unto him, and said, Ye know that the princes*
> *of the Gentiles exercise dominion over them, and they that are great*
> *exercise authority upon them. But it shall not be so among you:*
> *but whosoever will be great among you, let him be your minister.*
> MATTHEW 20:25-26, KJV

> *And whosoever shall exalt himself shall be abased; and*
> *he that shall humble himself shall be exalted.*
> MATTHEW 23:12, KJV

Perhaps there is a problem in the way the word minister is interpreted. It means servant, not ruler. I feel confident that God will let us know if the Gospel is to be altered in some way. He will tell us who is to be in charge if it is someone other than Jesus Christ.

These verses, in fact, all the words of Jesus leave no exceptions, no matter how important a bishop may be. If he will dominate, make rules and impose them on others, and excommunicate them for disobeying his rules or the church's rules, he has exalted himself above Jesus Christ. Without using words, he is saying that he is greater and has more authority than Christ. He exempts himself from the teachings of the Bible and assumes that his authority is greater than that of the Apostle Paul. And he portrays his righteousness to be greater than the righteousness of God.

It is very clear, if we will only open our eyes. No one is exempt. It doesn't matter if this ruler is your dad, your grandpa, your favorite uncle, or some kind hearted old gentleman. It doesn't matter if it is you. If anyone is ruling a church and keeping everyone in it under some church imposed form of righteousness, it is wrong. It is even more wrong to excommunicate those who wish to disregard it. No one is above, or by any means, exempt from the teachings of the Bible. It doesn't matter how righteous their righteousness may seem. If it is not congruent with the New Covenant, bought through the death and resurrection of Jesus Christ (the New Testament), it is simply false.

Satan was cast out of heaven because he believed his righteousness exceeded that of God (See Isaiah 14:12-15). He began to exalt himself over the other angels who were his equal. If God cast Satan out of heaven for this vain imagination, what will He do to those with such vain imaginations on earth?

Jesus came in a completely opposite manner; He came as a lowly servant. His exaltation was not at His own hands, but at the will of the Father God. Jesus did not come to set up an earthly kingdom, or to establish Himself as a great person. He came that the Father might receive glory.

Consider. The only son of the most high God came into this defiled earth. He was born to Nazarene parents. (Nazarene people of that time were considered a lowly sect.) He was born in a stable, probably a cave or a dugout type of animal shelter. He was raised with a simple lifestyle, someone we would consider to be a nobody. He worked in His earthly father's carpenter business. And beyond that, we know very little about His early life.

He was in His early thirties, possibly thirty-two years of age when he was baptized and began His recorded ministry of serving His fellow man. Why did Jesus wait until He was that old? You would think He could have begun His work at the age of twenty or so. That way, He could have gotten it over with more quickly, But He proved Himself as a servant, and a patient one at that. The example Jesus Christ left through His own ministry is the one that we must follow if we are to be called the sons of God. This is especially important if we are in any type of leadership position in the church. There are only two examples of leadership that we can choose from—Jesus Christ or Satan. There is no third example we can follow.

You will either choose to become a Christ-like leader who is humble and willing to serve the needs of your fellow man or ... or what? This means you serve both physical and spiritual needs. It also means you must not be swayed by his outward appearance, for if you do your part right, he will eventually look just fine. When you have ministered to his spiritual needs and he has embraced the truth, he will have no desires to dress and behave in a worldly way.

The other choice is to become a satanic influenced leader, to exalt yourself as lord over your church, and make rules that cause you to appear righteous. This will insure that your fellow man will look like a sinner if he does not look like you, dress like you, and follow your rules. You can choose the fear of man over the fear of God and keep everyone around you in line. You can choose to lie to your congregation by telling them that these rules are of God. If they disobey them you can tell them they are disobeying God's commandments. Wake up, O vain man! If God wanted you to have rules like that He would have made sure that they were included in the New Testament section of the Bible. Serving God is not some vague secret kept from everyone except the bishops.

The old covenant was bought about because of the sin of Adam and Eve. But God did not intend for it to be so from the beginning. That sin was not part of God's final and perfect plan and neither was the old covenant. The New Covenant fulfilled the Old and made God's redemption available to every person.

> *For if that first covenant had been faultless, then should no place have been sought for the second. For finding fault with them, he saith, Behold, the days come, saith the Lord, when I will make a new covenant with the house of Israel and with the house of Judah: Not according to the covenant that I made with their fathers in the day when I took them by the hand to lead them out of the land of Egypt; because they continued not in my covenant, and I regarded them not, saith the Lord. For this is the covenant that I will make with the house of Israel after those days, saith the Lord; I will put my laws into their mind, and write them in their hearts: and I will be to them a God, and they shall be to me a people.*
> HEBREWS 8:7-10, KJV

Because of sin, God made a covenant with His people until the day of redemption should take place through His Son Jesus Christ. Then He made a New Covenant. To make this covenant cost God the highest possible price, the blood of His only Son.

For as the blood of bulls and goats served in the old covenant, so did the much higher priced blood of Jesus Christ seal the covenant of the New Testament through which we may by faith be sealed into eternal life. It is only through this faith that we will ever come to God. All of our self righteousness (man-made forms of righteousness) is only as filthy rags in Gods eyes. God is not interested in seeing a certain set of clothes on our outward man. What He wants to see is our heart clothed with His Son Jesus Christ. Jesus said:

Judge not according to the appearance, but judge with righteous judgment.
JOHN 7:24, KJV

Therefore it is utterly inaccurate to say that if Christians do not dress in a certain way their prayers cannot be heard, or they will not make it into heaven. As long as one is dressed modestly and not in costly fashionable attire, who can say that it is not right? That being the case, what is left for the bishops to do in the church of Christ? There is plenty that truly needs to be done. If they would busy themselves doing what the Apostle Paul asked of them, things would be different

To better understand, let's look at the Greek definition of the word bishop.

(Strong's Greek Dictionary: *episkopo*; *episkopos* ep-is'-kop-os from 1909 and 4649 (in the sense of 1983); a superintendent, i.e. Christian officer in genitive case charge of a (or the) church (literally or figuratively):-- bishop, overseer.)

Thus, a bishop is to be a superintendent, an overseer, not a ruler or master, as some would have you believe. When this position is incorporated with Christ-likeness, we emerge with a beautiful picture of a loving superintendent of the Christian church body. He will carefully shepherd his assigned flock towards his master Jesus Christ. That picture seen in the context of 1 Timothy 3:1-5 would be a true blessing in any church. Notice verse 5 especially. "For if a man know not how to rule his own

If all of the bishops within the Christian churches would actually be required to conduct themselves as the Bible teaches, the Christian world would see an entirely different religion altogether.

house, how shall he take care of the church of God?" (Also see Titus 1:7-9). If all of the bishops within the Christian churches would actually be required to conduct themselves as the Bible teaches, the Christian world would see an entirely different religion altogether. If they were only to be ordained from a pool of such godly men, there would only be a very select few who could actually pass this exam. But if that were the case, the qualifications would have a very beneficial effect on the Church.

> *But a lover of hospitality, a lover of good men, sober,*
> *just, holy, temperate; Holding fast the faithful word as he*
> *hath been taught, that he may be able by sound doctrine*
> *both to exhort and to convince the gainsayers.*
> TITUS 1:8-9, KJV

"*Holding fast to the faithful word as he had been taught*" (Colossians 2:8), as in from the Bible—not as in the traditions of men, philosophy, vain deceit.

He could then both "exhort and convince the gainsayers." Notice the total absence in all of these verses the words rule" or "control" when addressing how a bishop is to lead his charge.

So many bishops look and act very plain and humble, yet inside they are filled with rage and bitterness. Dare to contradict their *ordnung* and they will pour out their satanic wrath against you. They see themselves as invincible, infallible, God-ordained rulers of the church. They never bother to align their doctrine with the Bible because the two don't line up. This should not be surprising to anyone. The Bible and the *Ordnung* are not one with each other, they conflict on so many points. Neither the Old Testament nor the New Testament support the ordnances of the modern day plain churches. They don't observe the Mosaic laws as God gave them in the Old Testament, and they don't follow the teachings of the New Testament because it teaches directly against one man ruling another (See Matthew 20:25-28) It teaches that we can no longer judge by the outward adorning or by plain clothes (See John 7:24), and that doctrines and traditional ordinances of man are not to be observed (See Colossians 2:8). However, the Bible does teach us that such false prophets should be shut up and disregarded.

> *For a bishop must be blameless, as the steward of God; not self-willed, not soon angry, not given to wine, no striker, not given to filthy lucre; But a lover of hospitality, a lover of good men, sober, just, holy, temperate; Holding fast the faithful word as he hath been taught, that he may be able by sound doctrine both to exhort and to convince the gainsayers. For there are many unruly and vain talkers and deceivers, specially they of the circumcision: Whose mouths must be stopped, who subvert whole houses, teaching things which they ought not, for filthy lucre's sake.*
> TITUS 1:7-11, KJV

Yet these Bishops continue in their deception. They refuse any Bible teaching that contradicts their traditional *ordnung*. They have exalted themselves above God, if such a thing is possible. They certainly have exalted themselves over and above His teachings.

> *Ye know that the princes of the Gentiles exercise dominion over them, and they that are great exercise authority upon them. But it shall not be so among you: but whosoever will be great among you, let him be your minister; And whosoever will be chief among you, let him be your servant:*
> MATTHEW 20:25-27, KJV

Anyone who exalts himself above others, for any reason, especially in a church setting, i.e., a bishop, minister, deacon, etc., exalts himself over Jesus. Jesus certainly did not do so, and neither did any of His apostles. How can someone who exalts himself above Jesus expect to be reconciled to God? Simply by conducting himself in a non-Christ-like manner he is without excuse. If even Satan, who at one time was an angel, was cast out of heaven for exalting himself over the other angels, what about these men?

These men do not know Jesus. If they did they would know about his personality. They would want to be like Him. But they are being used. Even though they don't realize it, they have become captains in Satan's army. In the early centuries, even until today, Satan instigated outward physical torture as means to rid the earth of his enemies, the Christians. This continues in many countries even today. But Satan has switched tactics in the United States and in a few other countries where such tactics are socially unacceptable. Instead he has planted his banner in the heart of the Christian church itself. He has ordained his servants to become bishops, elders, ministers, deacons, and other leaders within the church. And history is repeating itself. We are in the 21st century, and the grandchildren of the persecuted Christian Church have risen up to become the dictators within it. They rule and persecute their own without shame. Once again, as happened in the 1600s, it seems that God would have withdrawn Himself from the church had it not been for a remnant that would not bend.

Throughout the history of the one true church, the bride of Christ has remained faithful, and will forever remain intact, however small it may be. This persecution is no less than Jesus purging his threshing floor, as predicted by John the Baptist.

Whose fan is in his hand, and he will thoroughly purge
his floor, and gather his wheat into the garner; but he
will burn up the chaff with unquenchable fire.
MATTHEW 3:12, KJV

God is using these evil religions to do just that, to blow the chaff off of the wheat. To true Christians, it is known as persecution and it is a painful purging of Christianity. But it is not the end. Only through the power of the Comforter, the Holy Ghost will those select few remain faithful, but they will until Jesus comes again.

Chapter Twenty Two

A NEW STRATEGY

After a season of persecution one would think Satan would give up for a season. Do not be deceived, it is only a time for sharpening swords and training troops. New tactics are being set in place, new weapons are being tested, and (of course) new minions are being recruited. We are now in the third millennium—the 2000s.

(2012) Y2K is a distant fear. The world is in a recession, and the United States is no exception. Church attendance is on the rise. Perhaps a few new true Christians have been the result of this recession. But this will only last until Satan deploys another new tool of his. More money, better jobs, and no more fear of losing everything to the bank will cause people to become comfortable. Once again that cozy, relaxed and wealthy lifestyle for the people of the world comes back. The Christians will soon follow.

Of course, if the Christians were to be given all the wealth before the world gets it, the world would want to conform to Christianity. Give it to the world, however, and let the Christians see what they are missing, then convince them that they too can become wealthy, wealthy and Christian. It's an old, new strategy.

Satan will give the Christians exactly what they want and will withdraw himself from them until they have nearly forgotten about him. They will forget so completely, they will not remember Jesus. They will forget the persecution they once faced, and he and will give them something to keep their focus off of that blessed Redeemer Jesus Christ.

"I" says Satan "will give them back their money And lots of it. And freedom of religion, and an entire continent in which to practice it in.

Satan, who once was a taker of life, now comes in the form of a giver of an easy carefree lifestyle. The economy booms and money flows like milk and honey. Then he will once again remind the people how important money is to Christians. Church services will be held in enormous church houses and homes. People will justify their wealth by saying it is a blessing of God because of their goodness to Him. It's deceptive, because it's a lie. The Bible teaches us that we cannot serve God and Mammon (see Matthew 6:24). nor store up treasures upon the earth but in heaven (see Matthew 6:19-20). In fact, if God does choose to bless you with a lot of money, it is to give it to the poor. The rich man went to hell because he neglected to do so. (see Luke 16:19-31).

Satan, who once was a taker of life, now comes in the form of a giver of an easy carefree lifestyle.

But of course Satan has deceived many into believing that for a Christian to be rich is no less than God's blessing.

"Then," says Satan, "I will slay them all in their own selfish lusts. They will never forsake the comforts of the rich life to follow Jesus. They will even choose their own lives above all that Christ has to offer. Then, once again, I will insert my demons into the church to utterly destroy it by giving them what they really want. I will give them religion in the form of Christianity, with my minions as its leaders. Only this time I will keep a tight control over it all. I will see to it this time that nothing gets in my way. I will hide my design and my identity much better this time."

Satan has had over two thousand years to perfect his devices and sharpen his skills against the salvation of Jesus Christ and His followers. And now, like a seasoned general, he has become very crafty in his devises.

Says He, "I will come as a divine messenger of light, I will become as humble and plain, cloaked in humble clothing, and portrayed as righteousness, I will speak great soothing words to them if they will obey me without question. And those who would dare question my authority. I will rail and rage against. I will try to convince them that God hates them and their disobedience. I will intimidate and scare them into submission with the fear of hell. I will give them a form of righteousness that will make them to forget the blood of Jesus. They will forget salvation by faith and yield to fear and rules. I will hide the Holy Spirit from them, and give them rulers instead. They will not accept salvation by God's grace, but will conform to church standards of righteousness to escape their fear of hell.

"I will preach to them in long sermons and speak powerfully in a language that few can understand. I will convince them that by being good they might find favor with God. And I will persuade that by the way they dress the will be humble and pure and holy. I will pervert every rite given to them by God and his son Jesus. I will cause them to believe that their baptism will wash away their sins. I will completely remove Jesus from the ritual I so despise. Then I can replace Him with one of my minions. I will even hide the true definition of baptize from them (which is immersion, see Romans 6:3-4). I will convince them that their sins can only be forgiven through the intervention of a pope or a bishop. Then, effectively causeing them to deny the cleansing power of the blood of Christ. I will convince them that anyone who will not submit to my authority will be rejected, cast out and excommunicated (see Luke 6:22-23 and John 16:2-3).

"I will convince them that there is no hope for their souls unless they come crawling back to me and confess their deed. Then with a trembling voice full of contrition I will convince the rest of my servants that my judgment is necessary and that God hates those who do not obey me. I will blind their hearts so that no one ever desires to follow true Christians out of my church. I will pervert certain Bible principles into my own form of righteousness, and my rules will be very cunningly devised to be convincing to men. I will persuade them to follow my ordained men out of fear, by convincing them that these men were ordained of God to rule them. I will give them an endless list of rules that seem to be ordained of God. That will keep their focus off of the leadership of the Holy Ghost. I will convince them that no church can stand without rules and will use the Mosaic law of the Old Testament to convince them.

"In getting them to do all these things," said he, "I will definitely take their focus off of the Holy Spirit. I will cause them to fear the idea of salvation through grace by faith alone."

By doing this Satan will cause all of these dead religions to grieve the Holy Spirit and cause Him to withdraw Himself from them completely. Because of this they will have no concept of God's true plan of salvation.

This great deception of Satan has already begun and is now happening all around us. These great religions have grieved the Comforter who was sent to teach them all things (see John 16:1). The church in the mid 300s resorted to their own form of righteousness rather than seeking God's will. Like them, these churches will no longer heed the prophets and servants of God who are walking in their very midst. They cannot see Jesus any more than the Pharisees could, and for the same reasons. Their hearts have been blinded by their own religious deception.

This should not be surprising to those who read and believe the word of God, but sometimes is. Yet, notice what Jesus said.

> *And except that the Lord had shortened those days, no flesh*
> *should be saved: but for the elect's sake, whom he hath chosen,*
> *he hath shortened the days. And then if any man shall say to*
> *you, Lo, here is Christ; or, lo, he is there; believe him not: For*
> *false Christs and false prophets shall rise, and shall shew signs*
> *and wonders, to seduce, if it were possible, even the elect.*
> MARK 13:20-22, KJV

Jesus was not referring to men who come as roaring lions with huge swords and machine guns. He was speaking of false christs and false prophets who could just as easily be in your church as in any other. They just might be your preachers or bishops, and if they are teaching you false doctrine you are submitting yourself to the wrong authority. I have described much of their false doctrine in this book so that you can discern truth from falsehood. You need to get out from among them as fast as you possibly can (see 2 Corinthians 6:14 KJV).

If the one who is professing to be the keeper of your soul is more concerned about how you dress than the condition of your soul, he is not the one you should be following. He will cause you to fall into the snares of the devil. These false ministers have caused millions to be deceived across the centuries of history. They will never go away as long as God allows the world to stand. It is very dangerous to follow them blindly. It is dangerous to follow them at all.

> *Thus says the LORD: "Cursed is the man who trusts in man And makes flesh his strength, Whose heart departs from the LORD. For he shall be like a shrub in the desert, And shall not see when good comes, But shall inhabit the parched places in the wilderness, In a salt land which is not inhabited. "Blessed is the man who trusts in the LORD, And whose hope is the LORD. For he shall be like a tree planted by the waters, Which spreads out its roots by the river, And will not fear when heat comes; But its leaf will be green, And will not be anxious in the year of drought, Nor will cease from yielding fruit.*
> JEREMIAH 17:5-8, NKJV

Unfortunately, men continue to blindly follow these bishops and preachers and depend on them for salvation. Some rarely read the Bible, and some have even gone so far as to say that whatever their church leaders say is good enough for them. They think they will need no more than that.

Even some of these preachers will not read their Bible except to study for a sermon. In the Amish religion, this could mean only once a month, or even less. Who would want to follow the teachings of such an incompetent preacher? Yet, many people do, and they're doing it mostly out of fear. They have been taught from childhood that to leave the religion in which they were born is a one-way ticket straight to hell. If that were the case, all those martyred for their faith that we read about in the *Martyrs Mirror*, along with countless others including the apostles, would all have

God is no respecter of persons and the Gospel never changes.

gone to hell, At least as many of them who converted to Christianity from some other religion would have gone to hell.

God is no respecter of persons and the Gospel never changes, There is no difference between those who converted to Christianity from Catholicism during the Reformation period of the 1600s and those who convert to Christianity from Amish or any other apostate religion of the 2000s. Anyone who teaches otherwise is a false prophet and it is unwise to follow them or their doctrine. We must realize that even the greatest minister is only human and is by no means infallible. Yet that does not justify the absolutely sinful teachings of today's so called plain churches.

It is important that we submit ourselves to those who are set over us (see Hebrews. 13:17). But it is equally important that we only submit our souls to those who will watch over them in a true Godly manner. Nowhere in the Bible are we commanded to blindly submit our souls to some false prophet or to stay in a church that does not teach only sound Biblical doctrine.

Chapter Twenty Three

THE BODY OF CHRIST

In many ways, the Christian church has fallen into a sorry state of affairs. It has become formal, filled with man-made doctrine by which they identify themselves. Few churches have fellowship with others outside of their own little doctrinal world. This is not because other churches are non-Christians. It is because their man made doctrines don't agree. Christian groups bicker and fight over who is right and who is wrong. More often than not, both sides are wrong.

God's blessing has been removed from the church, and it has fallen into a state of dead religion. Many people only go to church because it looks good or feels good, not because they are on fire for God. They attend because that is what they do as Christians. The focus is placed on the church building, or group, or function. So, rather than being those who attend church because that is what a Christian does, many people attend church on Sunday mornings in order to be Christians, at least they attend some Sunday mornings.

We need to get our focus right again. We need to go back into the Bible and start over. We need to flush our minds of our preconceived ideas about how church life should affect our Christian lifestyle. Contrary to modern Christian theory, church is not the Christian life, even though it is a vital part of it. We need to be walking in holiness, as the Bible teaches. We need to be Christians first and church attendees second, rather than attending church in order to be Christian. We need to focus on becoming pure and holy before God rather than focusing on the church denomination to which we belong.

> *Pure religion and undefiled before God and the Father is*
> *this, to visit the fatherless and widows in their affliction,*
> *and to keep himself unspotted from the world.*
> JAMES 1:27, KJV

This verse is so very different from the teachings of most churches today. Some will visit the "fatherless and widows in their affliction" after church services on a Sunday afternoon. Heaven forbid that they should be caught skipping a church service to go amid the dirt and scum of society to minister to drug users and prostitutes.

No one was ever called to be a bench warmer or a Sunday Christian. While it is a good idea to be a part of a church, and to actively attend its services, the Bible does not teach that we should have church services every Sunday, or even on a regular bases. Christianity is a 24/7 lifestyle, Sundays included. We are all called of God to serve, but because of lukewarmness, few are chosen. If we expect to enter into heaven, we must become part of the Kingdom of God, or as Paul described it the body of Christ (See 1 Corinthians 12).We must become active in the service of the Lord.

Service to God is not about a church denomination, or how we dress, depriving ourselves of material things, or living in a colony to better serve one another. While keeping ourselves from the fashions of the world, not gathering worldly wealth to our selves, keeping ourselves from the world, or even living in a community may be part of the Christian life, we cannot build our doctrine on these things alone.

The Hutterites live in colonies and insist that to live in a colony is the only right way. The Amish have built their doctrine around Romans 12:2 … "be not conformed to this world …" and have made all sorts of stringent ordinances to try to keep them from the world. But they never realize that not being worldly depends on being spiritually transformed into a Godly soul. That soul neither cares for the world nor the things of the world. Any person who needs some law to keep him from the lusts of the world simply needs to be born again.

Wherefore if ye be dead with Christ from the rudiments of the world, why, as though living in the world, are ye subject to ordinances,
COLOSSIANS 2:20, KJV

To do the will of Christ is to love one another (See John 13:34-35, 15:12, 17, 1 Peter 1:22, and 1 John 3:11). It is not to dress a certain way or live a harsh and plain lifestyle, as if that should please God. To keep oneself from idolatry, adultery, things strangled, etc., as was required in Acts 15, is only showing love. Idolatry is a violation of love because it places things above God. Fornication is not showing love because we are robbing someone of their intimacy with a God approved partner. Partaking of things strangled is not showing love but it is also a form of idolatry and is the opposite of God's commandment. It keeps the life, which is represented by the blood, in bondage to the dead thing. The covenants ordained of God, both the old one, and the new one, required that blood flow out of the body. In dying for our sins, Jesus did exactly that. He shed His own blood.

For it seemed good to the Holy Ghost, and to us, to lay upon
you no greater burden than these necessary things.
Acts 15:28, KJV

We who wish to be part of the Kingdom must become servants, serving God by serving others. That is the only work that we can do to serve the Lord Jesus (See James 2:8). In so doing, we must not discriminate in race or color. But among the plainer religions, the chance of seeing a black person among them is very, very small. As of 2010, I have never seen a single black Amish Church member anywhere in the U.S. I was taught (wrongly) that for a white man to marry a black woman would be a grave sin in God's eyes. Yet Moses, whom the plain people idolize even more than Jesus, married an Ethiopian woman (See Numbers 12:1). They would much rather say the name Moses than Jesus. One might argue that this does not prove her color, but Jeremiah 12:23 suggests that an Ethiopian cannot change his color any more than a leopard can erase its spots. That is not the point.

The New Testament teaches that we are not to judge or discriminate.

There is neither Jew nor Greek, there is neither bond nor free,
there is neither male nor female: for ye are all one in Christ Jesus.
Galatians 3:28, KJV

Both black people and white, and people of every other race as well, will come before the judgment to receive their due reward. It then becomes apparent that God respects us all equally, and that He expects us to be able to fellowship together. If not, He would have made sure to include a note mentioning His desires in the New Testament.

The Apostle Paul used the human body as an illustration of how a church should function (See 1 Corinthians 12). So, we must remember that all the body parts, regardless or race or color, serve the head, who is Jesus. They have to be washed in the blood of the Lamb, not bound to some bishop or preacher. To serve the desires of the Head will never be a problem if we are true members of the body of Christ. A part that is cut off can no longer serve. Neither can a part of a foreign body know the desires of the head of the true body. The cut off members and the foreign body parts will not enter into eternal rest, because only one body will ever win that eternal rest. Eternal rest is for those members who have yielded themselves to Jesus and been washed in the blood of the lamb. Eternal rest belongs to those who have committed their lives to Him and are yielded members of His body, solely under His head or leadership.

> *To serve the desires of the Head will never be a problem if we are true members of the body of Christ.*

All true Christians are under his headship. Yet, the Head (Jesus) ministers to each member by knowing its needs and sending other members to minister to those who are distressed. A guest speaker at Camp Westly, North Carolina (revival meetings, 2009) gave a beautiful illustration of how the body of Christ ministers to the needs of one another. The speaker was from Africa. He told the story of how a scorpion stung him in his foot. The scorpion was quite large and the sting was very painful. Immediately after that happened, his entire body bowed down to the injured member to minister to it. The other foot, now on its own, went into overdrive, supporting the weight of his entire body as he hopped around in pain. Both hands reached down to hold this injured member. His entire body cried out in pain because this one member felt as if the entire body had been stung.

Now, according to the Apostle Paul, each member has its place and calling within the body of believers. Using this illustration, we might say the two feet represent the elders or bishops of a church body. This base of church leadership carries most of the load on itself for doing the will of the head. It carries the body as it travels through life. This is not likely to always be a pleasant or rewarding calling.

We might say the hands represent the ministers, or the deacons of the body or church. But neither the hands nor the feet will be able to properly function without the fingers or toes, and the fingers and toes need the nails. Without the nails, the fingers and toes are exposed. Those nails which are high maintenance and susceptible to built up dirt, are very important. But we must consider them properly. If they were to be ripped out, or beaten with a hammer, that would cause a great deal of pain to the body. It would temporarily, and possibly permanently, stunt the finger or toe and force the rest of the body to adapt.

In like manner, our internal organs, which we never see or want to see, are often neglected and unappreciated. They are not making any outward show, yet they are of the utmost importance, and they all must work together to be whole. The lungs are useless without the heart, and the heart without the lungs has no purpose. It would soon fail if the lungs were cast out. It would have no reason to pump if the arteries and veins were missing. The list goes on and on. In fact, we could write a book on this subject, but that is not the point.

The point is that we must consider each member within the body, even if it is one that never seems to do anything dramatic. The one who never preaches a great revival message or writes a life-changing book is important. The ones who pray in the background and the ones who support the poor are important. They may not be seen, but they are important. If we weed out and cut off everyone except those who do great or notable things, we are left with very little that can be called a body.

Take the nervous system for example. Few people, including myself, understand much about the nervous system. All we know is that it is connected to the brain somehow and sends signals to it from the rest of the body. When that African preacher got stung in the foot, guess who told the head about it? What relayed the message from the brain to the hands that the foot needed some immediate attention? It was that complex, often ignored, and misunderstood nervous system. Now if this were a serious snake bite and the nervous system turned a blind eye, what would have happened? "Oh," said the nervous system, "I'm not feeling up to paying attention to the whole body today." Or, what if it was just being too lazy to transmit the signals from foot to brain to hands and the rest of the body? Do you think the body would die? Of course it would!

Suppose, just for this illustration, that the body just ripped out the nervous system because it was angry with one of the feet for getting bitten. Or, suppose the body just decided to "play tough" and ignored the problem altogether. The imminent result would be death to the entire body.

We have all been born into this world with a predestined calling from the Father in heaven. No one was predestined to go to hell. To you, your calling may not seem as important as your neighbor's, but it is. Just because he's a handsome bicep muscle and you seem to fit the fingernail category doesn't determine your significance to the body.. If the body is called on to pick a pin off of the floor, can a bicep do that? No, that requires a fingernail. But a fingernail will not be able to do it without recruiting the assistance of the bicep. Together they will establish that the whole body can do what it is called to do.

Perhaps you remember how your dad, in his mid to late thirties, began to notice his hair with some concern when he combed it in the morning. That was probably not because he needed a haircut. It was because he realized his hair was leaving him altogether. We think of our hair as a high maintenance part of the body, and rightly so. Men are constantly in need of a haircut, and a woman requires a great deal more attention to her hair than a man does. Throughout our lives our hair seems to be high maintenance, but when it begins to leave us there is cause for anxiety.

Too many times one or another church member seems bothersome. But only when he leaves or dies do we realize how very important he was. Then we wish we could get him back and we probably regret the way we treated him when he was with us. No matter who we are, or who our brother is, God sees the significance of our calling. Others may not see it. We may not see it ourselves. But we should wake up to the fact that we have all been created equally in Gods eyes. He is no respecter of persons. To fail to acknowledge this is to wrongly judge God's most marvelous creation, which He created in His own image—man (See Genesis 1:26). He has redeemed all people, black and white, yellow, red and brown, by the blood of His only begotten son, Jesus Christ.

> *For as the body is one, and hath many members, and all*
> *the members of that one body, being many, are one body: so*
> *also is Christ. For by one Spirit are we all baptized into one*
> *body, whether we be Jews or Gentiles, whether we be bond*
> *or free; and have been all made to drink into one Spirit.*
> 1 CORINTHIANS 12:12-13, KJV

> *And they sung a new song, saying, Thou art worthy to*
> *take the book, and to open the seals thereof: for thou wast*
> *slain, and hast redeemed us to God by thy blood out of*
> *every kindred, and tongue, and people, and nation.*
> REVELATION 5:9, KJV

Amen, thank you Lord Jesus.

Chapter Twenty Four

THE "BUND"
THE OATH

U pon or immediately prior to their baptism, the Amish require
candidates to answer a series of questions that leads to an oath.
This, the clergy will hold over them for the rest of their lives. Among
the Amish, no one seems to know what the original or true way to do
this was. It is uncertain what they require, or even are allowed to require
these candidates to promise when they kneel before the local church
body to be baptized. Some bishops require candidates to promise to be
true to the Amish Church, its ways, and its traditions. Other bishops,
apparently having enough light to see the biblical error in such a vow,
simply and with a varying choice of words, require them to be faithful
to the church. This, more or less, is meant to describe the Kingdom or
church of Christ Jesus. In so doing they withhold the word Amish" from
the oath.

Now, here is cause for debate and rightly so. The *bund* or oath becomes
a fierce weapon to be used against those who would leave the Amish
Church. When a person makes this vow or swears this oath, he or she
promises to be faithful to that vow. If that person makes a vow promising

to be faithful to a certain church, in this case the Amish Church, what are the implications? And if later in life he decides to leave that church because of its doctrinal errors, is he bound by some biblical law?

When someone is baptized into the Amish Church, he is required to take such an oath – a *bund*. If that vow is made "to the church," rather than "to the Amish Church," it seems that leaving the Amish Church would certainly not be breaking that vow. But because the Amish clergy impose an oath at baptism, it is a serious matter; especially it that person later determines they should leave the church. Their honest concern is that they will suffer spiritual death if they do not keep this vow forever.

They will suffer spiritual death if they do not keep this vow forever.

When someone is baptized, and makes a vow to be faithful to the church and to keep the commandments of God, he is making a vow before God. Though he may not understand it, that vow is to the church of God, not to the Amish Church. Withholding the phrase "to the Amish Church," which is imposed by some Amish clergy, makes a difference. If someone has been required to make a vow to be faithful to "the church," as differentiated from "the Amish Church," that individual is definitely not breaking a vow by leaving. The church of Jesus Christ is universal and not limited to a specific denomination or group like the Amish Church.

What about those who vow or take an oath to "the Amish Church?" Many, perhaps most do so in complete ignorance of what is taking place. In some cases, they may not understand the German words used in the oath. When they are required to answer the questions, do they really know what they are agreeing to? Perhaps, and I am guessing, that many of the youth baptized into the Amish Church fall in this category. Either that, or they simply don't care enough to truly understand. But are they still responsible to keep the vow?

According to the Amish clergy, it makes no difference whether someone understood what was asked or not. If they answered yes to the questions in order to receive baptism, they are responsible to keep the vow no matter what. They reason that the individual could have paid attention in school and learned the language, or listened more carefully to the baptismal instructions.

Among the Amish, the children are taught from the cradle that the clergy is invincible and infallible. When they realize that the clergy actually is fallible, they quickly understand they have been deceived. That deception originated in the teaching of a false doctrine, and then trapping its membership under the "pain of damnation" (a term used by the Roman Catholic Church during the 1400s), and the fear of hell.

While I was still a part of the Amish, I became a member of the Masonic Lodge. That was a mistake perhaps. Nevertheless, it became the cause of serious grief to my Amish bishop. He demanded that I renounce my membership without delay. I actually did do that some years later, after I became a Christian. But renouncing, thus breaking the vow I made with the Masonic Lodge held far more frightening consequences than breaking the Amish *bund*. What they promised they would do to me if I decided to leave them was far worse than anything the Amish ever threatened to do to me. Yet, my conclusion is not about the pain or the curses with which I was threatened by either group. The point of my story is to demonstrate that the Amish do not believe their own threats when it comes to the breaking of vows. If they did, they would not have ordered me to renounce my vow to the Masonic Lodge and resign.

According to their teaching, it doesn't matter if a vow is justifiably righteous or not. A vow is a vow, and cannot be broken. That is what they say when their vow is being trespassed upon. If they actually believed that, they would never have asked my wife to leave me when I decided to leave the Amish Church. They were the people who joined us in marriage. They caused us to promise to live together "till death do us apart." Yet they were willing for my wife to break her vow to me when I decided to leave them.

I clearly see this promise as a righteous vow, based on Scripture (See Mark 10:11-12). What I cannot accept is that men become dictators and make rules which require other men to take unjustifiable vows. I cannot accept that they impose on others a promise to align themselves to a certain church when they (the clergy that enforces these man-made vows) cannot prove they themselves believe in them. The Bible clearly teaches us that there is only one God and we are to serve Him alone, for a man cannot serve two masters.

Then saith Jesus unto him, Get thee hence, Satan: for it is written,
Thou shalt worship the Lord thy God, and Him only shalt thou serve.
MATTHEW 4:10 KJV

God never commanded us to take any vows. If he was intent on us making one it would be in the New Testament. Instead, the New Testament teaches differently.

But above all things, my brethren, swear not, neither by heaven,
neither by the earth, neither by any other oath: but let your yea
be yea; and your nay, nay; lest ye fall into condemnation.
JAMES 5:12, KJV

True, this verse does not justify someone who broke a vow. It only addresses those who insist that their church members make one binding them to a certain church denomination.

The Apostle Paul was himself subject to a vow he had made before he was saved. The Bible does not tell us what that vow was. Neither is that necessarily important. What we do know is that he shaved his head because of that vow (See Acts 18:18). Then in Acts 21:23-26 we read of four other men who had taken a vow, and Paul joined with them in days of ritual purification so that the Jews not be stirred against him.

In the book of Numbers, we can read a lot about vows and how the Israelites were instructed to make, keep, and/or free themselves from vows. We simply have no reason to believe that a vow made to an apostate church should be honored if it jeopordizes one's spiritual well being. These types of church oaths are just another implement of terror, employed by an apostate church clergy to entangle its membership into its web.

We simply have no reason to believe that a vow made to an apostate church should be honored if it jeapordizes one's spiritual well being.

My conclusion is simply this: A biblically justifiable vow made to God should be kept. A vow made to any man, so long as it does not interfere with, change, or in any way conflict with or infringe upon the Word of God, should be kept in honor of one's fellow man. However, any vow made because of an intention to bind an individual to a certain church (namely the Amish Church) is not a biblically justifiable vow. No one should be bound to that vow by any measure.

But Peter and John answered and said unto them,
Whether it be right in the sight of God to hearken
unto you more than unto God, judge ye.
ACTS 4:19, KJV

Chapter Twenty Five

THE UNEQUAL YOKE

God called Abram to leave his father and mother and go to a strange land (See Genesis 12:1). We don't read that God spent a lot of time explaining why. Neither did Abram question God or argue with Him. He simply obeyed in faith. It is quite likely that Abram's parents thought he was a bit crazy, traveling into the wilderness on what may have seemed like a whim. But he obeyed God.

In later years, after God changed his name, God called Abraham to offer his only son Isaac as a burnt offering (Genesis 22:2). Again, Abraham obeyed Gods command by faith, without question. We then read how God spared Abraham's son (Genesis 22:12) once Abraham had demonstrated his loyalty to Him.

Like Abraham, we are often required to sacrifice areas of our lives, proving to God that we are loyal to Him alone. Often, if we are required to leave behind our families for the sake of the Gospel, we are rewarded over and over again.

And every one that hath forsaken houses, or brethren, or sisters, or
father, or mother, or wife, or children, or lands, for my name's sake,
shall receive an hundredfold, and shall inherit everlasting life.
MATTHEW 19:29, KJV

Sometimes God tests our loyalty to Him by requiring us to leave a church we have been raised in. This is not always the case, but it does happen. Of course, leaving a church because of strife or rebellion is not what Jesus meant in Matthew 19:29. Leaving because we see the error in their doctrine is not rebellious, but it can be difficult.

To truly follow God by faith could require us to forsake certain family members who are not willing to follow us in our journey out of bondage. This by no means implies that we can or should leave them in anger or carry bitterness toward them, as some do. They blame every problem, even small ones they are not willing to repent from, on the way they were raised. This is self pity, nothing more. To hold bitterness is not honoring to one's father and mother, something the Bible teaches us we should do.

However, as members of the bride of Christ, we must realize there may come a time when even our own children may be called by God. Then they will have to go and engage their God-given talents in whatever endeavor God has ordained for them. If we force our children or our church members to remain in the church we determine, we just might be intruding in Gods sovereign plan. Far too many talents are wasted because of some selfish parent or bishop. Sometimes people have elevated themselves into such powerful positions they simply refuse to let go. When they do, God is being robbed of the glory He alone deserves.

Many souls lie in waste because people are forced to remain in an apostate church or cult, bound by an unrighteous oath they took. Sometimes they only took that oath to please a domineering parent or a bishop. Now they lie in waste like a fallow field. They are this way because their God given talents have never had the opportunity to freely shine. They are rotting away.

Satan must rejoice to see this happen. He craftily intends for these talents to rust away, rather than become useful tools to build up God's kingdom. Far too many churches that profess to be unworldly and submissive have completely missed the point. They have gone far afield to establish their own authority rather than accept the simple plan of salvation ordained by Jesus Christ. They build upon the traditions of their dead forefathers rather than on the Gospel. And when they do so, they become completely rebellious. We cannot build on the foundations of man or his ideas of righteousness

> *Jesus saith unto him, I am the way, the truth, and the*
> *life: no man cometh unto the Father, but by me.*
> JOHN 14:6, KJV

We will all answer for ourselves at the judgment day. Those controlling dictators in the clergy will not be there to answer for you on that day. They will not make excuses for you or explain how good you were.

We will be on our own, each man to answer for himself. Only what was done for Christ will stand the test of fire at judgment day. No one will be able to use his plain clothes, his long beard, his broad suspenders, or his big hat. All of this will mean nothing to God. Those things cannot be found in the Bible. In fact there is no dress code in the Bible that pertains to righteousness. People who rely on dress codes will take their chances with the words of Jesus.

> *But all their works they do for to be seen of men: they make broad*
> *their phylacteries, and enlarge the borders of their garments.*
> MATTHEW 23:5, KJV

This would seem to eliminate any church imposed dress code for that matter. The things that will stand the fire of judgment are not worn outwardly. They are found inside our hearts. They bear the sign of the cross. They have witnessed true Christian baptism and have not persecuted Christians, but rather bear the scars of persecution. Their deeds have ministered to the poor without anyone else noticing. They have spread the Gospel message of Jesus Christ unfailingly. Their deeds have been done in love, never exalting themselves or forcefully imposing their views on others. These Christians have experienced the truth of what our Lord said of them.

> *Blessed are ye, when men shall hate you, and when they shall*
> *separate you from their company, and shall reproach you,*
> *and cast out your name as evil, for the Son of man's sake.*
> LUKE 6:22, KJV

> *He that loveth father or mother more than me is not worthy*
> *of me: and he that loveth son or daughter more than me is not*
> *worthy of me. And he that taketh not his cross, and followeth*
> *after me, is not worthy of me. He that findeth his life shall*
> *lose it: and he that loseth his life for my sake shall find it.*
> MATTHEW 10:37-39, KJV

These are the worthy deeds that shall withstand the trying of the fire in that great and dreadful day of our Lord.

> *Even so Lord come!*
> REVELATION 22:20

> *Every man's work shall be made manifest: for the day*
> *shall declare it, because it shall be revealed by fire; and*
> *the fire shall try every man's work of what sort it is.*
> 1 CORINTHIANS 3:13, KJV

26

Chapter Twenty Six

...When Men Shall Speak Well of You

Woe unto you, when all men shall speak well of you!
for so did their fathers to the false prophets.

Luke 6:26, KJV

Over and over throughout history men have risen up in defense of God's word. They have proclaimed the truth of the Gospel and in so doing have stood against the doctrines of men who selfishly perpetrated false doctrine. These men were never popular and never were well-liked among the worldly minded religious leaders. Time and again churches have been raised up, with their people on fire for God. But then the fires began to cool, and with that cooling come rules and the doctrines of men. These are followed shortly by spiritual death.

When loyalty to God is lost and shifted to a demand for loyalty from the membership in order to defend it, and man-made doctrine rises, the end is near. Compare any modern day religion with the Bible and you will see that many of them have reached that point. They are more to be compared to the Pharisees of Jesus time than the followers of Jesus. He prophesied that His followers would be hated, persecuted, martyred, and evil spoken of, and they have been. Thousands of men and women have lost their lives because they stood for the truth. They chose to suffer and even to die, rather than give in so they would be well spoken of.

They were often hated because their message convicted others of their sin, others who would rather lash out than repent. Many of these men came from less than desirable backgrounds. They were not all that popular in the first place. Thus, after they were saved, redeemed by the blood of Jesus, it was easy not to care whether they were well liked or not. The message they carried was far more important than popular opinion. The opportunity to see souls come to Christ was far more rewarding than to be well spoken of by the high and mighty of society.

These men were not going to be stopped by any king, president, magistrate, secret police, pope, bishop, parent or brother. The more they were hated, the bolder they became. They quickly realized that their old friends were of no help to their cause. Rather, they were a hindrance to their calling in the Kingdom. The less they had, the more they were free to depend on God. Subsequently they realized they could also depend on their Christian brothers for support and comfort.

To be excommunicated from a dead religion is a blessing. It simply cuts off another tie with the world. In fact the stricter the shunning, the more one is forced to reach out to Christ for comfort. Therefore, one's walk with the Lord Jesus becomes more fulfilling. It also helps him to discern more clearly between wolves in sheep's clothing and true sheep. He no longer feels the need to defend someone he thinks may return the favor.

> *Excommunication from a dead religion is a blessing.*

If only these dead religions would wake up, they would see that they are writing their name in the books of history by the way they act toward true Christians and persecute them. Unfortunately, they are writing their name right alongside the Pharisees and the Roman Catholic Church. They are committing the same sins against the same faith.

> *So he carried me away in the spirit into the wilderness: and I saw a woman sit upon a scarlet coloured beast, full of names of blasphemy, having seven heads and ten horns. And the woman was arrayed in purple and scarlet colour, and decked with gold and precious stones and pearls, having a golden cup in her hand full of abominations and filthiness of her fornication: And upon her forehead was a name written, MYSTERY, BABYLON THE GREAT, THE MOTHER OF HARLOTS AND ABOMINATIONS OF THE EARTH. And I saw the woman drunken with the blood of the saints, and with the blood of the martyrs of Jesus: and when I saw her, I wondered with great admiration.*
> REVELATION 17:3-6, KJV, EMPHASIS ADDED

Why would the blood of saints make someone drunk? Look at what happens to men when they are drunk. Their senses grow numb to what is going on around them. Things they once realized were sin no longer seem to be so. Rather, they seem right and good. Their consciences grow dull and bother them far less, if even at all. And when they are drunk, they do abominable things they would not do if they were sober.

This is what happens to a church when it begins to persecute its Christian members. It gets worse and worse. The punishments that are handed down become more gruesome. The crowds grow larger and more blood thirsty. They grow drunk on the blood of the saints, and like an adulterous wife, they deal treacherously with God (See Ezekiel 16).

It is for this reason that God has hardened their hearts and stopped up their ears. They will not be able to see Jesus, or even to hear the truth when His servants walk in their midst. (See Isaiah 6:10.) They cannot hear real Christians, men whose pants and beards do no match their own preconceived ideas of righteousness.

The Pharisees missed the promised Messiah because they expected Him to be one of them, an arrogant self-righteous, pompous Pharisee. But the Messiah came exactly as promised, and if the Pharisees had been studying God's word for what it says, they would have recognized Him. Instead, they were perverting the Scripture to suit their own thinking. They were not doing what God called good deeds or acts of righteousness. Instead, they were busying themselves with their self righteousness and making sure everyone else was walking their line. How typical of today's self righteous religions that are missing the Messiah's messengers. Since they don't have the outward appearance of someone they assume to be a righteous man, they don't receive them.

> *Remember the word that I said unto you, The servant is not greater than his lord. If they have persecuted me, they will also persecute you; if they have kept my saying, they will keep yours also.*
> JOHN 15:20, KJV

Yet, the Gospel was written in such a way that they cannot understand.

> *Therefore speak I to them in parables: because they seeing see not; and hearing they hear not, neither do they understand. And in them is fulfilled the prophecy of Esaias, which saith, By hearing ye shall hear, and shall not understand; and seeing ye shall see, and shall not perceive: For this people's heart is waxed gross, and their ears are dull of hearing, and their eyes they have closed; lest at any time they should see with their eyes, and hear with their ears, and should understand with their heart, and should be converted, and I should heal them.*
> MATTHEW 13:13-15, KJV

27

Chapter Twenty Seven

WHY THE GOSPEL ANGERS

And this is the condemnation, that the light has come into the world, and men loved darkness rather that light, because their deeds were evil. For everyone practicing evil hates the light and does not come to the light, lest his deeds should be exposed. But he who does the truth comes to the light, that his deeds may be clearly seen, that they have been done in God.
JOHN 3:19-21

The truth has always been painful to those who were trying to hide something, especially sin in their lives.

And ye shall know the truth, and the truth shall make you free.
JOHN 8:32, KJV

No one who is free from hidden sin has any reason to be offended when presented with the truth, and the Gospel is undeniably the ultimate truth. This is especially true when it is presented as a gift instead of as a hammer. If you present the true Gospel to a true Christian he will most likely be excited that you have found the strait gate mentioned in

Matthew 7:13, like he has. But to those who are living in sin, the Gospel will bring conviction—not necessarily condemnation, but conviction. Unfortunately, most people do not want to be set free from their sin. Without realizing it, they are hoarding their sin to themselves and refusing to let it go. In refusing to acknowledge it, they are refusing to let the blood of Jesus wash them clean. It is unfortunate, but they are vain and proud. They don't want their sin to be exposed, and when they are presented with the Gospel, they are all forced to make a choice. We all are.

If someone chooses to accept the Gospel, it calls for repentance and surrender to Christ, then a new life begins. The other choice is to reject this Gospel. People generally do not like to be put in a position where they are forced to make that choice. They would be much more at ease if an annoying evangelist would just go away. But he is the one in front of them, God's visible messenger. Suddenly, he becomes the one at fault for their sinfulness. He is not offering a made-up message or a fairy tale. He has received his message from his Father in heaven. The sinner does not know that. Neither does he know the Father or acknowledge the message is from God. Therefore the evangelist finds himself being the persecuted one.

Interestingly, this happens far more when evangelizing religious folk who think they have it all together than when evangelizing the unreligious. The heathen, the no holds barred, honest in his sin unbeliever often appreciates that a Christian should have enough concern for him to reach out in love.

There is another type of evangelizing individual, one who uses the Gospel more like a hammer than like a love letter from God. That person also gets some persecution, but he is only getting what he deserves. The

Gospel is a message of love, and grace, and mercy. It should be delivered in that way.

The religious man only uses Jesus to justify his fleshly lusts, his financial greed, his religious ideas, and his hidden sin. Many profess that they have accepted Jesus. They might even believe it in their hearts. But when they are confronted by the evangelist who presents them with the truth, they become rude, arrogant, and sometimes downright mean. This clearly separates the religious from the Christians. It is the same thing that separated the Pharisees from Jesus Himself.

> *Wherefore by their fruits ye shall know them.*
> MATTHEW 7:20 , KJV

"By their fruits" is so often interpreted to mean "by their outward appearance." The Amish even preach that a person with a pure heart will dress plain. The question that comes is this. Which standard of plain can be counted as righteousness? Will it be the Amish standard? Perhaps the Mennonite standard is better, the Hutterite standard, or the Islamic one?

To confuse the issue, we know that there are many different Amish standards, many different Mennonite standards, and some various Islamic standards as well. None of them is exactly like the standards of the Pharisees in Jesus time, or even like those of the orthodox Jews today. Yet, we have only one set of Scriptures—one Bible. Not an English Bible and a German Bible, a Latin Bible or a Dutch Bible. That is why Jesus said:

> *Judge not according to the appearance, but*
> *judge with righteous judgment.*
> JOHN 7:24, KJV

The Gospel fits all races, all nationalities, males and female alike. Dress codes cause strife. When dead religions bicker and fight over who is right, even though none of them are, they have lost their ability to bring people to Jesus. Church standards have caused more splits, more enmity, and more strife than any other cause. They have also caused more blindness, and are the main reason so many churches have ceased to evangelize or do mission work effectively.

Try going to the Copper Canyons in Mexico where there is serious pagan darkness and much demonic influence. There the women wear floor length, multi layered dresses and scarves that cover their entire head except for their faces. These head coverings are not some transparent veil either. What would happen if you were to convert them and then dress them in Amish clothing with tight form-fitting dresses? What if you made sure that the hems of their dresses were 8 inches from the floor, no more, no less, and not floor length? What if you removed their big cloth head covering and put an Amish covering on their head? What would they do? These pagan women turned Christian would be embarrassed to be seen in public. And perhaps they should be.

We must be able to look beyond our culture and tradition to be able to minister what really counts.

Take a plain religion into the city and try to convince anyone to become that type of Christian. They will not buy into it any more than those women from Mexico would. Christianity and religion like this cannot work together. As Christians, we will not be able to do the work our Lord Jesus commanded if we try to mix religion with our own ideas. Our plain ways simply do not mix with other cultures. We must be able to look beyond our culture and tradition to be able to minister what really counts. We must reach into the hearts of people, not try to convert them to plain ways.

The truth is that any man who holds Christ higher than his own religion will not likely get angry when presented with the Gospel. Yet, even if we wrote the truth in bold black letters on a white sign and held it right in front of their faces they would refuse it.

> *He hath blinded their eyes, and hardened their heart; that*
> *they should not see with their eyes, nor understand with*
> *their heart, and be converted, and I should heal them.*
> JOHN 12:40, KJV

Time will go on, and people will continue to uphold their religion higher than the simple Gospel message of Jesus Christ. They cannot comprehend how only by faith in Jesus can we find grace in God's eyes. So they continue to insist on trying to help things along with their religious ideas as years turn into decades, decades into centuries, and centuries into millenniums. They never realize that in doing that they are essentially saying the work of the cross was not sufficient without their input.

The Roman soldiers were not the last ones to slap Jesus in the face. It will continue to be so, and it will separate the wheat from the chaff. Godly evangelists, missionaries, bishops, elders, pastors, deacons, and apostles, will continue to do the work which they have been called to do. Like Daniel and his friends, Shadrach, Meshach, and Abed-Nego, they will stand against the crowd. Like so many of God's prophets, including Isaiah, Jeremiah, and even God's own son Jesus Christ, they will be counted worthy. The twelve apostles (except for John) all lost their lives for this most holy cause. Thousands of Anabaptists lost their lives because they spoke the truth to religious men that hated the truth. These were men who refused to shut up, refused to sugarcoat or dilute the truth for anyone, no matter what. They were men and women filled with God's Spirit and were willing to count everything but loss for the Gospel.

That same spirit still lives today in the hearts of men and women who have completely sold out to Christ. They have sold out to the One who bought them with the highest price ever paid. Like those who trod the way before them, they will not shut up. They will not stop until their hearts stop beating. They refuse to dilute the truth, paint it in shaded colors, or make it other than what it is. Not for you; not for anyone. They have left family, friends, homes, jobs, businesses, and churches. They are being scorned, mocked, shunned, rejected, despised, and given over to Satan by excommunication, but neither Satan nor the religious leaders have any power over them. They are too close to God.

They are being imprisoned, tortured, and killed and still they tarry on. Nothing has ever stopped them and nothing ever will. As long as there are Christians on planet Earth, they will continue to proclaim God's truth. These are your fathers and mothers, your brothers and sisters, your sons and your daughters. They have a calling from God and will carry it through. If they must suffer heat, or cold, or dust, or mud, wild beasts, or hunger, or thirst, or pain, they will endure. But their greatest enemy will always be their fellow man, the religious man who professes to be the chosen of God but really does not know Him.

> *As long as there are Christians on planet Earth, they will continue to proclaim God's truth.*

www.ingramcontent.com/pod-product-compliance
Lightning Source LLC
Chambersburg PA
CBHW051823090426
42736CB00011B/1623